Legal Risk Management for Associations

Jerald A. Jacobs and
David W. Ogden

Legal Risk Management for Associations

A Legal Compliance Guide for

Volunteers and Employees of Trade and

Professional Associations

American Psychological Association
Washington, DC

Published by
American Psychological Association
750 First Street, NE
Washington, DC 20002

Copies may be ordered from
APA Order Department
P.O. Box 2710
Hyattsville, MD 20784

Typeset in Century by Easton Publishing Services, Inc., Easton, MD

Printer: Wickersham Printing Company Inc., Lancaster, PA
Cover designer: Kachergis Book Design, Pittsboro, NC
Technical/production editor: Valerie Montenegro

Library of Congress Cataloging-in-Publication Data
Jacobs, Jerald A.
    Legal risk management for associations : a legal compliance guide for volunteers and employees of trade and professional associations / Jerald A. Jacobs and David W. Ogden.
        p.   cm.
    Includes index.
    ISBN 1-55798-304-6 (acid-free paper). — ISBN 1-55798-312-7 (pb. : acid-free paper)
    1. Trade and professional associations—Law and legislation—United States.
I. Ogden, David W.   II. Title.
KF2902.J323   1995
346.73′064—dc20
[347.30664]   95-5868
                                                                                           CIP

Printed in the United States of America
First edition

Contents

Preface

This book, *Legal Risk Management for Associations*, is based upon a similar one prepared originally for the American Psychological Association (APA), a 124,000-member national scientific, professional, and public interest society in the field of psychology. Several years ago, the APA's Committee on Legal Issues, composed of attorney-psychologists, identified a need for a book explaining the principles of law and government policy that affect that Association. The Committee stipulated that the guide must be in plain English, that it must relate the legal and policy principles to concrete but hypothetical APA factual situations, and that it must be comprehensive enough to engage the sophisticated volunteer and staff leadership of the Association, all of whom are PhD psychologists. The APA's book, *Legal Risk Management: A Guide for Volunteers and Staff of the American Psychological Association* was published in 1993 and has been distributed and used extensively by the APA as well as by many related associations in the field of psychology.

In adapting the APA's legal compliance book for promulgation in the broader trade and professional association community, it was necessary to make extensive changes. References to the APA and to psychology have been removed, of course. Several chapters have been added and several, extensively rewritten. The entire manuscript has been edited for continuity and pertinence to typical or average trade and professional associations—large, medium, or small; and national, state, or local.

The purpose of this book is to educate volunteers and employees of associations who hold positions of authority and responsibility regarding the context in which legal liability issues can arise for membership organizations. The purpose is not to provide legal advice, which requires the evaluation of specific factual situations in the light of the law applicable to those situations. In short, although the book can make associations better clients, it cannot substitute for the advice, judgment, and experience of association attorneys.

We hope and trust that the book will be of assistance to, and used by, associations of all kinds and sizes in managing successfully the unique legal risks raised for association volunteers and employees.

The authors are deeply indebted to Dort Bigg, Esq., Director, APA Legal Affairs Department, for his consistent wisdom, encouragement, and assistance in this project.

Jerald A. Jacobs
David W. Ogden

How to Use This Book

This book, *Legal Risk Management for Associations*, is intended to assist volunteers and employees who have positions of responsibility and authority for trade or professional associations in

- avoiding violations of the law,
- protecting their association's future, and
- accomplishing their association's goals and objectives effectively and with increased confidence that legal problems will not interfere.

Associations of all kinds, whether large, medium, or small in size and whether national, state, or local in scope, are affected or potentially affected by a host of laws and regulations at the federal, state, and local levels. Many of the applicable rules are highly technical and nonintuitive; common sense is simply not a sufficient guide to avoiding legal liability. Violations of the law, whether intentional or unintentional, can have severe consequences for the association and for the individuals involved. Familiarity with the pertinent portions of this book is therefore crucial for those who work with associations in any capacity.

This book is *not* intended as legal advice or as a substitute for consultation with an association's legal counsel whenever legal liability issues arise. It is intended to help association volunteers and employees identify potential legal problems and seek legal assistance if needed. When associations incur legal liability, it is more often from ignorance than from malicious intent. It is hoped that this book will prevent legal violations from occurring inadvertently. *The best advice for association volunteers and employees is to contact the association's senior executives or legal counsel whenever one has questions about the law as it applies to association policies or programs, or whenever one is concerned that association-related activities may be in violation of the law.*

This book was prepared based primarily on federal law. State and local governments frequently have different or additional legal requirements for associations. The book presents only a general overview of legal risk avoidance for trade and professional associations. It concentrates on liability issues for those associations and avoids legal issues related more to association management and administration such as tax exemption, lobbying and political filings, and so on. The book should not be relied upon as a comprehensive treatise or manual on all of the laws affecting all types of associations.

How to Find Pertinent Portions of the Book

Portions of the book applicable to one's own activities on behalf of a trade or professional association can be located in two ways.

First, each chapter contains a brief section titled Who Is at Risk? This section is meant to help the user discover whether the legal principles discussed in the chapter are relevant.

Second, the structure of the book is intended to facilitate the location of pertinent subject matter. The book is divided into six parts, and each part is further divided into chapters.

What Is Included in the Book

Part I, Legal Issues for All Volunteers and Employees, includes chapters on "Loyalty and Conflicts of Interest"; "Respecting Confidentiality"; "Apparent Authority"; "Discrimination by Federal Grantees"; "Antitrust Generally"; and "Defamation." Everyone involved with an association should review the six chapters of Part I.

Part II discusses eight specific ways in which an association might be engaged in the "self-regulation" of the trade or profession represented by the association. Separate chapters are devoted to "Advice and Endorsements"; "Business and Professional Ethics"; "Accreditation and Approval"; "Guidelines, Advisories, Models, or Recommendations"; "Professional Specialization, Certification, Recognition, and Listing"; "Product Standards, Testing, and Certification"; and "Membership." All association volunteers and employees considering action related to these areas should review the chapter pertinent to the contemplated activity.

Part III discusses legal compliance in professional practice programs; the chapters are "Fees, Reimbursement, and Modes of Practice" and "State Licensing." Association volunteers and employees considering initiatives affecting these areas should consult the appropriate chapter in this section first.

Part IV is on legal compliance in business price and cost programs, and it covers a particular risk for trade associations, conversations at meetings. The chapters are "Surveys of Prices or Costs" and "Discussions at Meetings."

Part V pertains to legal compliance in association publishing activities, including copyright issues. This chapter should be reviewed by those engaged in publishing activities on behalf of an association.

Part VI has as its subject the various employment issues that can arise in an association, particularly "Employment Discrimination" and "Wrongful Discharge." Volunteers and employees of associations who have responsibilities for engaging, reviewing, compensating, assigning, or terminating association employees should become familiar with these chapters.

Arrangement of the Chapter

With a few exceptions because of the particular subject matter, each chapter is divided into five sections. First comes a general overview of the legal issues surveyed in the chapter; second, Who Is at Risk?; third, a more detailed summary of governing legal principles; fourth, some hypothetical scenarios intended to illustrate the application of the principles to the day-to-day operation of an association; and fifth, suggestions on how to minimize risk to oneself and one's association.

Appendixes

There are three appendixes following the book's 20 chapters.

Appendix A is a sample policy for dealing with conflicts of interest that may arise among volunteers or employees in the operations of a trade or professional association. It is consistent with the discussion of this subject in chapter 1. Each association may have differing needs for explanation or emphasis in promulgating a conflicts of interest policy, but this one is general enough that it can likely be adapted for use by most associations.

Appendix B is a sample set of guidelines on apparent authority. As discussed in chapter 3, the U.S. Supreme Court has determined that an association can be held responsible for the illegal acts of volunteers or employees, even when the leadership of the association was not aware of those acts, did not approve of them, and did not benefit from them; all that is necessary to bind the association is that the volunteers or employees appeared to outsiders to be acting on behalf of the association. Many associations have found it useful to develop special guidelines for volunteers and employees addressing this unique apparent authority risk for associations.

Appendix C is a sample statement of antitrust compliance policy and direction that may be used or adapted by a trade or professional association. Some associations find it helpful to include a statement such as this in their bylaws or other governing documents and to distribute the statement periodically at meetings of the associations' governing boards or committees.

Further questions about legal compliance should be addressed to the association's senior executives or legal counsel.

Part I _____

Legal Issues for All
Volunteers and Employees

Introduction

The chapters in Part I discuss legal concerns that permeate the operations of nearly every trade or professional association. Everyone involved with an association should be familiar with the issues discussed herein. Chapters 1 and 2 are very important because they discuss the obligations that volunteers and executives have to their associations. Chapter 3 makes clear that individuals may legally bind an association and impose substantial legal liabilities upon the association, even if the association has not approved or ratified their unlawful conduct. It provides guidelines for avoiding liability based upon the theory of "apparent authority." Chapters 4, 5, and 6 discuss three areas of the law that affect virtually every aspect of association functioning: laws against discrimination, antitrust violations, and defamation. Familiarity with each of these six chapters can be considered a basic duty of all association volunteers and employees.

1

Loyalty and Conflicts of Interest

What Are the Duties of Care and Loyalty?

A trade or professional association is typically a nonprofit, tax-exempt membership organization that conducts its affairs through a governance structure of association leaders. The governance structure is usually composed of boards, committees, divisions, sections, task forces, and other groups of elected or appointed volunteers who are responsible for making, recommending, or approving association policy and procedure throughout the organization or at least a segment of the organization. Employed staff of the association assist in these endeavors and then are responsible for implementing the association's policies and procedures. All of the association's volunteers, and all of its employees, have legal responsibilities to the association.

Those in positions of responsibility and authority in the governance structure of the association, both volunteers who serve without compensation and employed staff, have a "fiduciary duty"—including duties of both "care" and "loyalty"—to the organization. In simple terms, this means that they are required to act reasonably and in the best interests of the association, to avoid negligence or fraud, and to avoid conflicts of interest. In the event that the duties of care and/or loyalty are breached, the person breaching the duty is potentially liable to the association for any damages caused to the association as a result of the breach. This fiduciary duty is a duty to the association as a whole. Even those who only serve a particular committee, task force, division, or other segment of the association owe the fiduciary obligation to the organization.

Who Is at Risk?

As noted, all volunteers who play any role in the governance of the association or any of its segments, and all employed staff, owe duties of care and loyalty to the association and are potentially liable to the association should they fail to act consistently with those duties.

What Legal Principles Govern the Duties of Care and Loyalty?

1. **The duty to act in the best interests of the Association.** This duty is very broad, requiring volunteers and employees to exercise ordinary and reasonable care in the performance of their duties, exhibiting

honesty and good faith. Thus, an association volunteer or employee has the duty to exercise due care when acting on behalf of the association, to attempt to avoid generating legal liability for the association, and to attempt to further the association's interests rather than the individual's own interests or the interests of any other party. The duty also imposes an obligation to protect any confidential information obtained while serving in the fiduciary role with the association. (See chap. 2, "Respecting Confidentiality.")

2. **The duty to avoid conflicts of interest.** The duty of loyalty encompasses a duty to avoid conflicts of interest and to provide undivided allegiance to the association's mission. A conflict may exist when a volunteer or employee of the association participates in the deliberation and resolution of an issue important to the association while the individual, at the same time, has other professional, business, or volunteer responsibilities outside of the association that could predispose or bias the individual one way or another regarding the issue. In these situations, it is typically *not* enough for the individual to be aware of the conflict and to attempt to act in the association's best interest despite the conflict. On the contrary, for many conflicts, full disclosure to the organization and refraining from participation in the organization's deliberation and resolution of the issue (i.e., recusal) are required to remedy the conflict. For serious, visible, continuing, or pervasive conflicts, withdrawal from the volunteer or employed position, or from the outside conflicting responsibility, may be required. It is important to be sensitive to and to avoid *apparent* conflicts of interest as well as actual conflicts.

In the context of an association's self-regulation programs (i.e., professional or business ethics enforcement, professional certification or academic accreditation, product standards and certification, and similar programs), the duty to avoid conflicts of interest also mandates that all individuals acting on behalf of the association not have conflicts with respect to the interests of the persons, products, or entities that are the subjects of the particular activities or proceedings in which the individuals are involved. Thus, for example, a volunteer or staff member of an association committee considering certification of a particular entity's services must not participate in consideration, deliberation, or resolution of the matter if the person has relationships or interests that (a) give the person an economic stake in the outcome, (b) enmesh the person with any party or witness in any way, or (c) afford the person prior knowledge about the matter that causes the person to prejudge its appropriate outcome. No volunteer or employee should serve in the same matter in both an investigatory and an adjudicatory role.

3. **Corporate Opportunities Doctrine.** The duty of loyalty specifically prohibits competition by an association volunteer or employee with the association itself. Those individuals may generally engage in the same "line of business" or areas of endeavor as the association, pro-

vided it is done in good faith and without injury to the association. One form of competition that is not permitted, however, is appropriating "corporate opportunities." A corporate opportunity is a business prospect, idea, or investment that is related to the activities or programs of the association and that the individual knows, or should know, would be in the best interests of the association to accept or pursue. An association's volunteer or employed representatives may take advantage of such a corporate opportunity independently of the association only after it has been offered to, and rejected by, the association.

Hypothetical Scenarios Concerning Fiduciary Duties

The following scenarios are fictional. They are designed to illustrate the nature of legal risks faced by association volunteers and employees in the area of fiduciary duties. Any resemblance to actual persons or to institutions or entities is completely unintentional.

Example 1: Negligently Damaging the Interests of the Association

A technical committee of a national association of manufacturers is divided into subcommittees that operate state-by-state to encourage governments to adopt acceptable environmental regulations applicable to the manufacturers. The chair of the committee learns that members of the subcommittee for the State of Amsterdam have agreed that they will simultaneously raise prices if the State adopts particular unfavorable environmental regulations. Although the chair knows that this conduct would very likely violate the antitrust laws and could potentially implicate the association and impose substantial liability upon it, the chair neither attempts to discourage the activity nor notifies the association's executive staff or legal counsel. The scheme is uncovered by the government, which conducts an investigation and adjudication including the association as a target; ultimately, the association pays a substantial fine and pays six-figure defense costs. The association learns that the chair of its technical committee had knowledge of the scheme in advance and failed to act. The chair could be held liable by the association for its fines paid to the government and for its defense costs.

All volunteers and employees have a duty to act reasonably in the association's best interests. If one has reason to believe that the association's interests are in jeopardy, one must notify appropriate personnel promptly and take whatever additional steps are suitable to avoid the liability for the association.

Example 2: Engaging in Self-Dealing

A member of the governing board of a state professional society owns a substantial interest in a small, emerging computer software company but is not actively involved in its management. Without disclosing this relationship with the company, the individual suggests to the association's chief employed officer and chief financial officer that they consider this company as the vendor for a large software purchase contemplated by the association. When the matter comes to the Board for a choice among several competing bidders for the contract, the member argues strenuously and successfully that the contract should go to this company, still not disclosing her ownership interest in the company.

The board member's failure to disclose a business interest and to withdraw from the association's consideration of the matter is an obvious violation of the member's fiduciary obligation. It could subject the person to liability to the association, to its members or to its creditors.

Anyone with a personal stake in an association decision should disclose that interest and recuse oneself from deliberation and decision on the matter.

Example 3: Acting Despite a Personal Relationship That Creates a Conflict

A member of a national trade association is assigned to serve on a three-member business code of ethics hearing panel that is reviewing a complaint of deceptive advertising against a corporate member. After receiving the materials on the complaint, the member realizes that a distant relative is the complaining party in the matter. The member considers recusal—withdrawing from the matter—but decides that it is unlikely that anyone will learn of the relationship with the complainant and believes that it will not affect objective decision making. After a conference with the other two panelists, the member concludes that there has been an ethics code violation and votes to drop the company from membership. The company later learns of the relationship and successfully sues both the panelist and the association. The association is advised by legal counsel that it has a strong claim against the member on the panel for breach of the duties of loyalty and care, but, convinced of the panelist's good faith, declines to sue.

Again, all doubts concerning conflicts should be resolved in favor of full disclosure. Often recusal will be advisable as well.

How Does One Minimize Risk to Oneself and to the Association?

1. Place the association's interests first in dealings on the association's behalf. Be alert to possible opportunities and risks, and promptly inform appropriate personnel concerning those opportunities or risks.
2. Be alert to possible conflicts of interest and to circumstances that could

create even the appearance of a conflict of interest, and at a minimum disclose those conflicts before taking part in any deliberations or decisions on subjects where conflicts or possible conflicts exist.

3. Be aware that recusal may be appropriate where an actual or apparent conflict of interest exists.

4. Preserve the confidentiality of information acquired in one's capacity as a volunteer or employee of an association wherever it appears that the information is proprietary to the association.

5. Do not appropriate corporate opportunities available to the association.

6. Adoption of a policy governing the conduct of governance volunteers and staff relative to addressing conflicts of interest may help avoid problems in this area. A sample conflicts of interest policy is provided in Appendix A.

2

Respecting Confidentiality

What Is the Obligation to Respect the Confidentiality of Information?

Association volunteers and employees are occasionally required to have access to confidential information or data. The need for confidentiality may arise because confidentiality is in the best interests of the association or because disclosure of information or data could injure individuals or organizations. In some cases, confidentiality is required by law. In others, disclosure could risk liability for defamation. (See chap. 6, "Defamation.")

Examples of confidential information or data maintained and used by associations include

- information generated by confidential self-regulatory processes such as standards setting, certification and accreditation, or business or professional code enforcement;
- opinions and other privileged information received from inside or outside legal counsel or other consultants;
- certain kinds of tax information and financial statistics;
- employment and compensation information or data that will be unduly invasive of personal privacy; and
- trade secrets or confidential commercial information generated through the business endeavors of the association or shared with the association by outside business concerns on the condition of maintenance of confidentiality.

As part of the fiduciary obligation that they owe to the association (see chap. 1, "Loyalty and Conflicts of Interest"), volunteers and employees are required to maintain in confidence all information and data that the organization considers and treats as confidential. They are not permitted to disregard or overrule the association's determinations of the need for confidentiality. The obligation to maintain confidentiality continues indefinitely.

Who Is at Risk?

Any association volunteer or employee who discloses confidential information risks imposing liability on the association because the association, in certain contexts, has a legal duty to maintain confidentiality. Even where the association has no such duty, the release of confidential information may harm

the association, and the individual who disclosed that information may therefore be liable to the association for breach of the individual's fiduciary obligations.

What Legal Principles Govern the Duty to Respect Confidentiality?

The duty to maintain confidentiality extends to materials and information
designated as confidential and also to information that the volunteer or employee should know the association would not wish to have revealed to others.
The duty prohibits these individuals from purposefully disclosing confidential
information and requires them to act with due care to avoid the inadvertent
disclosure of confidential information.

Information Designated as Confidential

Information may be designated as confidential in various ways. Documents
may be marked confidential, such as documents that contain attorney–client
communications or an attorney's legal opinions or factual research (called
"attorney work product"). Information may be transmitted in "executive session" or in confidential minutes of executive sessions of meetings. Alternatively, categories of information, such as self-regulation program proceedings
and records, may be designated as confidential in the bylaws or other rules of
the association.

　　Where legitimate reasons exist for confidentiality, association volunteers
and employees should formally designate information as confidential. This
privilege should not be overused, however. An association requires a high level
of openness to function properly and with due regard for the interests of its
members. Before executive session is invoked, a strong reason for confidentiality should be identified and agreed upon. Generally, the reasons will be
among those set forth in the first paragraph of this chapter. Executive session
may *not* appropriately be invoked to exclude a member of the governing board
or executive staff, or a designee of the member, from *any* association meeting.
There may, however, be extraordinary circumstances in which legal or procedural requirements mandate that such an individual be absent. For example,
debate on code enforcement against a volunteer member by a committee or
board on which the member sits or debate on contract negotiations with a staff
member by a committee or board that the staff member administers would
constitute such circumstances. (See chap. 1, "Loyalty and Conflicts of Interest.") Where a matter is required to be kept confidential, it may not be disclosed
within or outside of the association, except within the association to the extent
necessary to accomplish the association's legitimate objectives.

Information Not Designated as Confidential

The duty of confidentiality extends to information *not* designated as confidential as well, wherever the individual should know that the association would not wish to have the information released to a third party.

Hypothetical Confidentiality Scenarios

The following scenarios are fictional. They are designed solely to illustrate the nature of legal risks faced by volunteers and employees of associations.

Example 1: Disclosure of Attorney–Client Information

During executive session at a professional association's Board of Directors meeting, outside legal counsel informs the Board, based on confidential information provided to counsel, that the association faces serious legal risks in connection with its recent enforcement of certain features of the association's code of ethics. Later, one volunteer member of the Board relates this legal opinion to colleagues at the professional practice where the member works. Litigation ensues over the code enforcement. During the litigation, the plaintiff's attorney happens to learn about the disclosure of legal counsel's opinion beyond the Board of Directors and seeks to force the association to reveal the substance of the opinion. The court finds that the disclosure by the Board member has waived the attorney–client privilege, orders the association to disclose it, and permits it to be used against the association in the litigation. As a result, the association decides that it must enter into a very unfavorable settlement, costing the association a substantial sum.

Attorney–client information should be protected to the utmost and revealed only to those persons specifically authorized to learn of it by counsel.

Example 2: Disclosure of Information Pertaining to Employment and Compensation of Association Employees

An association volunteer leader serves on a committee responsible for monitoring the association's staff compensation structure. After completing the term for this position in the association, the individual becomes a volunteer leader in a second association. Using knowledge of the compensation paid to the chief executive of the first association, the volunteer spearheads a successful effort to recruit that chief executive to the second association, at a slightly higher salary. The first association sues the former volunteer leader, proves that it lost its chief executive due to the volunteer's abuse of confidential information obtained while the volunteer had fiduciary duties to the association, and recovers from the volunteer a substantial award to compensate it for its cost of replacing the chief executive.

Example 3: Inadvertent Disclosure of Confidential Information

An association employee working on the association's product certification program takes files home to work on them. The employee leaves a briefcase containing the files on the subway, where it is recovered by a reporter for a newspaper. The reporter reviews the files and learns from them that a well-known new product will not be certified by the association because it may be unsafe. The paper runs the story, and the company that makes the product sues the association for negligently releasing confidential information to the public. The association settles out of court for a substantial amount. The employee resigns under pressure after the association considers, but rejects, the possibility of seeking reimbursement from the employee.

Great care must be taken to safeguard the confidentiality of sensitive materials.

How Does One Minimize Risk to the Association and to Oneself?

1. Carefully preserve the confidentiality of any information that comes into one's possession and that is designated by the association as confidential. Confidential information should not be shared with any unauthorized person.
2. Before disclosing to anyone association information obtained through volunteer or employment responsibilities for the association where the information is *not* formally designated as confidential, consider whether the information is such that it would be in the association's interests to preserve confidentiality. If confidentiality may be in the association's best interests, or if the question is close, refrain from disclosure.
3. Do not disclose to third parties, or to persons within the association who do not need to know, information provided by the association to its attorneys in confidence or the substance of legal opinions provided to the association by its attorneys.
4. When entrusted with confidential records or information, take great care to avoid inadvertent disclosure.

3

Apparent Authority

Limitations on the Authority of Volunteers and Employees

In 1982, the U.S. Supreme Court determined that an association is liable for antitrust violations arising from the activities of its volunteers or employees, even when the association does not know about, approve of, or benefit from those activities, as long as the volunteers or employees appear to outsiders to be acting with the association's approval (i.e., with its "apparent authority").

The famous decision is *American Society of Mechanical Engineers, Inc. v. Hydrolevel Corp.* In it, the Supreme Court made clear that associations are to be held strictly liable for the activities of volunteers and of employees that have even the apparent authority of the associations. The imposition of liability is intended as a warning to associations that they must adopt and follow procedures to ensure that antitrust violations, even unauthorized ones, do not occur.

Many associations have promulgated procedures, or incorporated procedures into other governing documents, to provide guidance for volunteers and employees on the limits of their authority to act on behalf of the associations. Sample apparent authority guidelines are included in this book as Appendix B.

Who Is at Risk?

The Supreme Court's apparent authority doctrine has applicability to all volunteers and employees of an association, as well as bodies or entities integral to the association's governance structure (councils, boards, divisions, committees, subcommittees, ad hoc groups, task forces, work groups, etc.). These include all leaders and staff of an association. State and local chapters or affiliates of larger federations of associations can also be affected by the apparent authority doctrine.

What Legal Principles Govern the Law of Apparent Authority?

Even if an association volunteer or employee does not *in fact* have authority to act in a particular manner on behalf of the association, the law will nevertheless hold the association liable if third parties reasonably *believe* that the volunteer or employee had authority. The law thus requires an association to take reasonable steps to ensure that the scope of its agents' authority is clear to third parties.

Hypothetical Scenarios Concerning Apparent Authority

The following scenarios are fictional. They are designed solely to illustrate the nature of legal risks faced by association volunteers and employees.

Example 1: Boards and Committees

A medical association establishes a committee to review pronouncements on health care issues made by other organizations, both governmental and private, and to publish abstracts of those pronouncements for the information of the society's membership. The mission statement for the committee makes clear that the committee is to review and possibly abstract pronouncements of other organizations, not to issue such pronouncements itself. To facilitate the committee's dealings with other organizations, the association permits the committee to print stationery bearing the committee's name and the name of its members and chair. The chair of the committee has championed the use of a particular diagnostic drug, called Formula A, which is in competition for recognition by the profession with a newer drug, called Formula B. The chair receives an inquiry from Orange Star Insurance Co. about Formula B. The chair directs a lower level association staff member to respond on committee letterhead that Formula B "has been deemed potentially unsafe and ineffective, as well as unnecessarily costly." Orange Star begins refusing to reimburse for the use of Formula B, and several other insurers follow suit.

The manufacturers of Formula B sue the association and win a substantial antitrust judgment against it.

An association must avoid permitting circumstances to exist in which an improperly motivated member could commit violations of law in the association's name. Following common sense and the sample apparent authority guidelines in Appendix B will help avoid such problems for an association.

Example 2: Conflict of Interest

A trade association's Task Force for Approval of Testing Companies has as its mission reviewing applications from local testing companies and approving those whose composition and procedures render them fit, in the view of the Task Force, to provide valid testing of the safety of the industry's products for the benefit of commercial users of the products. Approval by the Task Force confers a substantial advantage in attracting clientele for the local testing companies. Member A of the association's Task Force is from the tiny state of Old Amsterdam and in fact operates a testing company generally recognized as a model for the nation. Member B is from the neighboring state of New Rotterdam and also operates a well-recognized testing company in that state.

The Task Force divides its work among subcommittees and issues letterhead stationery to each of its members upon which to issue approval decisions. It specifically directs its members to recuse themselves in any case presenting a conflict of interest. Members A and B serve on a two-person subcommittee.

Member A learns that a new testing company has been formed, seeking to do business in both Old Amsterdam and New Rotterdam. Member A ensures that the application is referred to her subcommittee. Members A and B then conspire to reject the application, despite knowing that they had a direct financial conflict of interest, and despite the fact that the application would likely have been approved on the basis of a neutral review. The new testing company thereafter fails to attract a sufficient clientele and goes out of business. Later, the investors in the defunct testing company, learning that Members A and B composed their own subcommittee and that they had a conflict of interest, sue the trade association for a violation of their right to due process and for an antitrust conspiracy. They recover a substantial sum from the association. The association could hold Members A and B legally accountable to the association for breach of their duties of care and loyalty.

An adequate system of checks and balances must be instituted before an association takes any action that could cause adverse impact on members or third persons. Centralized control of stationery and of authority to act are very important.

How Is Risk Reduced for an Association and Its Leadership?

1. **Standards, guidelines, and credentials.** Extreme care is necessary in the development of standards, guidelines, or credentials that affect economic interests or competition. When such documents might have effects upon prices or fees charged by members, scope of practice or modes of practice for professionals, compensation or reimbursement, sales of products or professional engagements, assignment of tasks or titles, or other economic or competitive factors, the antitrust laws are implicated. (See chaps. 10, "Guidelines, Advisories, Models, or Recommendations," 11, "Professional Specialization, Certification, Recognition, and Listing," and 12, "Product Standards, Testing, and Certification.")

    Standards, guidelines, and credentials must state who is authorized to interpret them, such as special committees or the governing board. Formal interpretations must be issued in writing. Extreme care must be used in formulating any statements regarding standards, guidelines, or credentials that are expected to be relied upon by association members or by others, whether or not there are specific enforcement mechanisms related to the standards, guidelines, or credentials.

    If the standards, guidelines, or credentials do include enforcement mechanisms, there must be provisions to ensure that due process is afforded to those affected, including the opportunity for appeal. (See chaps. 8, "Business and Professional Ethics," and 9, "Accreditation and Approval.")

2. **Correspondence and statements.** Official correspondence and statements, whether issued explicitly or implicitly by or on behalf of an association, must be approved in advance.

    Other correspondence or statements must not be on the association's letterhead, and, if they could possibly be interpreted as issued by or on behalf of the association, a disclaimer indicating that they are not made by or on behalf of the association may be warranted.

3. **Meetings.** All meetings of an association must be scheduled in advance if practicable, have agendas circulated to attendees in advance, be open if practicable, and have written minutes prepared and circulated to attendees.

4. **Adoption of apparent authority guidelines.** Adoption of such guidelines (see sample guidelines provided in Appendix B) may assist association staff and volunteers in minimizing risk pertaining to apparent authority.

4

Discrimination by Federal Grantees

What Is Discrimination?

Discrimination is the failure to treat all persons equally where there is no
reasonable distinction between those favored and those not favored, and where
the basis for the discrimination (sex, race, etc.) is prohibited by law. Discrimination includes unfair treatment or denial of normal privileges because of a
person's race, color, sex, age, national origin, religion, or physical or mental
disability. A number of federal, state, and local statutes forbid discrimination
in housing, employment, public accommodations, education, grant programs,
and various other areas. Many associations are recipients of various federal
grants and are thereby prohibited from discriminating against individuals in
any aspect of their operation on the basis of their race, color, sex, age, national
origin, religion, or mental or physical disability. (Although discrimination on
the basis of sexual orientation violates the laws of several states and the
District of Columbia, it does not violate federal law.) This prohibition includes
an obligation not to discriminate with respect to membership, volunteer leadership opportunities, enforcement of business or ethics codes, academic or other
accreditation, or any other aspect of associations' policies or programs. This
chapter does not address employment discrimination, which is covered in chapter 19.

Each agency that administers federal funds is required to promulgate
regulations to enforce the prohibitions against discrimination. If an association
that receives federal grants were to discriminate unlawfully, it could lose its
federal funding and be required to pay damages to the individual(s) who was
discriminated against.

Who Is at Risk?

Because federal law prohibits an association grant recipient from discriminating on the basis of prohibited characteristics in any aspect of its operations,
every program of that association can potentially incur liability for the association and for the individual who discriminates. Discrimination is unlawful
with respect to any right, privilege, benefit, entitlement, standard, penalty,
or indeed any other aspect of the association's activity.

What Legal Principles Govern the Law of Discrimination by Grantees?

It is unlawful for a federal grantee to discriminate intentionally against an individual on the basis of any of the prohibited grounds. It is also unlawful to engage in any practice that has the effect of excluding members of a protected class. This sort of exclusion effect can result from a seemingly neutral requirement, classification, procedure, examination, and so forth. Similar standards apply to nonemployment discrimination as apply to employment discrimination (e.g., pregnancy discrimination, sexual harassment, reasonable accommodation of disabilities; see chap. 19).

The federal agencies that provide grant funds to associations will conduct periodic compliance reviews of the recipient associations' programs (whether or not those programs are federally assisted), as well as investigate any complaints of discrimination. Under the Department of Health and Human Services (HHS) regulations, for example, every application for federal financial assistance must be accompanied by affirmative assurances that affected programs or facilities will be conducted or operated in a nondiscriminatory manner. Recipients are also required to prepare and maintain compliance reports and submit them upon request to the responsible HHS official (e.g., recipients should maintain racial and ethnic data showing the extent to which members of minority groups are beneficiaries of, or participants in, federally assisted programs). Affirmative action programs are acceptable under the HHS regulations and may even be required where past discrimination is found.

Hypothetical Scenarios Concerning Discrimination Claims

The following scenarios are entirely fictional. They are offered only to illustrate the nature of legal risks faced by volunteers and employees of associations that receive federal grant income.

Example 1: Disability Discrimination

A national professional association, as part of a research grant program administered by HHS, requires applicants for research funds to complete a written examination. One of the applicants for the program is visually impaired. She contacts the association's administrator of the examination to inquire about having the examination prepared in braille or, alternatively, taking an oral examination. The examination administrator informs the applicant that oral examinations may not be substituted for written ones, and further, that the examination is unavailable in braille. The administrator states that the applicant is free to have a reader accompany her to the examination at her expense. The applicant arranges for a reader to accompany her and to read the questions to her. The applicant answers the questions by using her brailler and then having the answers transcribed. The applicant, however, is given no additional time to complete the examination. The applicant fails the examination and does not qualify for research funds.

The applicant subsequently files a complaint with HHS. HHS investigates and finds that the association violated the Rehabilitation Act of 1973 and the Americans with Disabilities Act (ADA) by failing to reasonably accommodate the applicant's visual impairment. After HHS threatens to withdraw federal assistance from the research program, the association agrees to allow the applicant to retake the examination, which it further agrees to have prepared in braille. The applicant passes the examination and is qualified to receive research funding. The association provides the researcher with a reader and a braillist to assist her in the research. HHS investigates again and this time finds that the association is in compliance with the Rehabilitation Act and the ADA; federal assistance is not withdrawn. In the course of the proceeding with HHS, the association expends considerable time of volunteers and employees, as well as consultants' fees, in resolving the matter satisfactorily.

Example 2: Race Discrimination

As part of a routine compliance review, HHS discovers that racial minorities are underrepresented in the highest category of membership, for Fellows, of a large, prestigious scientific association that receives federal grant money from HHS. The federal agency conducts an investigation and finds no evidence of intentional discrimination. It determines, however, that the scientific association's practices for recruiting applicants to the Fellows category result in a very low number of minority applicants for this category of membership. Instead of withdrawing federal assistance, the HHS helps the association establish a minority recruiting program in order to increase the number of minority membership applicants in the Fellows category. The association also implements a limited affirmative action program to remedy the past discrimination.

Example 3: Sexual Harassment

Tom is the chair of a committee of a state engineering association that receives federal grant funding. On numerous occasions, Tom has approached Mary, a member of the committee, and asked her to go to dinner with him. Mary has consistently refused these invitations, telling Tom that she is not interested in any involvement with him outside of the association's committee work. Tom persists in these now clearly unwanted propositions, making Mary extremely uncomfortable. Mary is considering dropping out of the committee but instead contacts an executive of the association to complain about Tom's conduct. The association's Executive Committee discreetly impanels a task force to investigate the situation; it soon confirms the conduct and asks Tom to halt his behavior. The Executive Committee threatens to terminate Tom's chairmanship if he continues to harass Mary. Tom then apologizes to Mary for his inappropriate behavior and conducts himself in a professional manner for the duration of the program. Mary had been considering filing a complaint with the federal agency that administers the grant funds and also pursuing a private cause of action but decides that these actions are now unnecessary because the association has effectively handled the situation.

How Can an Association Grant Recipient Minimize Risk?

Although it is impossible to avoid all claims of discrimination, an association that is a federal grant recipient can significantly reduce its risk of these claims by implementing the following guidelines:

1. Carefully review all tests, examinations, criteria, and so on to determine whether any could have a disparate impact on members of a protected group.
2. Audit recruiting and application procedures to determine whether any could have a disparate impact on members of a protected group. Develop strategies to effectively recruit members of protected groups.
3. Maintain data on participation in association programs by members of protected groups.
4. Carefully audit compliance with the Rehabilitation Act and the ADA, especially in the area of reasonable accommodation.
5. Be particularly sensitive to discrimination issues if you are involved in administering federally assisted programs that have specific mandates regarding discrimination (i.e., grants, financial aid, education, research, etc.).
6. Cooperate (with the assistance of legal counsel) in any discrimination investigations by federal agencies. HHS regulations, for example, instruct investigators to attempt to obtain voluntary compliance prior to imposing sanctions.
7. Promptly investigate any complaints of discrimination, including harassment. Take appropriate steps to remedy any problems.
8. Above all, be sensitive to every individual's right to not be discriminated against based on race, color, ethnicity, sex, national origin, religion, disability, marital status, or sexual orientation, and to the association's duty to avoid engaging in any discriminatory practices or conduct.

5 _____

Antitrust Generally

What Is Antitrust Law?

The federal antitrust laws (principally the Sherman and Clayton Acts) and the trade regulation statutes (principally the Federal Trade Commission Act) are intended to promote open and fair competition in all commercial endeavors. State antitrust laws generally follow the federal pattern and have the same objectives. Since the 1970s, it has been clear that the federal antitrust laws apply with full force to the learned professions, including architecture, law, engineering, medicine, dentistry, and psychology.

Trade and professional associations are organizations of members, many of whom compete with one another. Therefore, virtually any action that such a trade or professional association takes, and particularly actions that involve the attempted private regulation of a business or profession, may raise antitrust issues. Many of these actions are perfectly lawful. There is a broad range of lawful activities for associations to take relating to standard setting, certification of products or professionals, dispute resolution, and other forms of business or professional self-regulation. Great care must be taken, however, to ensure that an association's activities do not fall within the special unlawful categories established by the courts as "anticompetitive." The courts consider an action to be anticompetitive when, on balance, it raises prices or fees or lowers the quantity or quality of available goods or services. Prices and fees, in fact, are a particularly sensitive area. Any action of an association that directly raises, lowers, or stabilizes prices or fees has the highest risk of antitrust scrutiny and the greatest potential penalties. Even action that may only indirectly affect prices and fees, such as association-promulgated arrangements on terms and condition of sale, warranties, limitations on the extent or type of advertising, and hours of operation, can also be expected to attract antitrust scrutiny of the association.

Violations of the antitrust laws may be prosecuted by the federal government, either civilly or criminally, and by injured private persons or entities. Courts may award injunctive relief against violators and may require violators to pay victims three times the financial injury actually suffered (called "treble damages"), plus their attorneys' fees.

Who Is at Risk?

An association and its individual volunteers and employees who cause the association to violate the antitrust laws are potentially at legal risk. Antitrust is one area in which there are many precedents for both civil and criminal action brought not only against association entities but also against association members and staff when there is evidence that they participated personally in antitrust violations. Specific areas of concern for associations include self-regulation programs (Part II of this volume), professional practice programs (Part III), and business price and cost programs (Part IV). Separate chapters of this book address the application of antitrust principles to these specific areas of concern and provide instructive hypothetical scenarios as well as specific guidance on ways to avoid exposure to antitrust liability.

What Legal Principles Govern Antitrust Enforcement?

Violations of the antitrust laws fall into two basic categories: (a) actions that are unlawful without regard to their actual impact on competition (called *per se* violations) and (b) actions that are not necessarily unlawful, but may be so, depending on their actual impact on competitive conditions (called *Rule of Reason* violations).

Actions that are likely per se unlawful include the following:

- agreements fixing prices or fees or setting floors or ceilings on prices or fees;
- agreements to boycott competitors, suppliers, third-party payers, or customers/patients/clients;
- agreements among competitors dividing or allocating markets; and
- agreements coerced by a provider with a dominant market position tying the purchase or provision of one product or service to the purchase or provision of another product or service.

Any other agreement—including resolutions of, or other measures taken by, an association of competitors—may violate the antitrust laws under a Rule of Reason analysis if its effect is generally to raise prices or fees or to reduce the quality or quantity of available goods or services.

It is very important to understand that the antitrust laws can be violated by mutual understandings or other informal arrangements falling far short of a formal contract or written resolution. Individuals may violate the antitrust laws, or implicate their associations in antitrust violations, by using the associations to facilitate their undertaking anticompetitive arrangements among themselves, even without invoking any of the formal mechanisms of the association. Indeed, an association may be held responsible for anticompetitive conduct by its volunteers or employees who only appear to be acting in the name of the association but, in fact, violate its policies. (See chap. 3, "Apparent Authority.")

How Does One Minimize Antitrust Risk for the Association and for Oneself?

Users of this book should refer to the specific sections that address particular areas of association policies and programs that may pose antitrust risks. Generally, however, the following guidelines should be observed:

1. Avoid agreements, resolutions, or other actions—formal or informal, written or unwritten—that relate to commercial prices or professional fees.

2. Avoid agreements, resolutions, or other actions—formal or informal, written or unwritten—that restrict nondeceptive advertising.

3. Avoid agreements, resolutions, or other actions—formal or informal, written or unwritten—that constitute a boycott (i.e., a collective refusal to deal), except to the extent that the boycott is motivated purely by political (i.e., noneconomic) concerns. Legal counsel should be sought with respect to any proposed action that could be characterized as a boycott, whatever its motivation.

4. Avoid agreements, resolutions, or other actions—formal or informal, written or unwritten—that could be construed as representing a division or allocation of markets among competing economic actors.

5. Avoid agreements, resolutions, or other actions—formal or informal, written or unwritten—that tie the provision or purchase of one good or service to the provision or purchase of another good or service.

6. Avoid any other action that appears likely to have the effect of raising prices or fees or reducing the quantity or quality of goods or services that are available.

7. Adoption of an association antitrust compliance policy may assist association staff and volunteers in understanding the need to comply with the antitrust laws. A sample antitrust compliance policy is provided in Appendix C.

6

Defamation

What Is Defamation?

Defamation is the oral utterance ("slander") or written publication ("libel") of false facts or false implied facts damaging to an individual's, entity's, or product's reputation. Typically, defamation may be committed even by those who believe that they are communicating the truth. The defamed individual may sue anyone who publishes, prints, or repeats the defamation and, depending on the circumstances, may recover from the speaker sums of money to compensate for the harm to reputation and to "punish" the speaker as well. In some circumstances, "privileges" apply that may protect the speaker from legal liability.

Who Is at Risk?

Publishing and other communications activities are among the major endeavors of most associations regardless of size or kind; associations therefore face the acute and persistent legal risk of defamation. Those responsible at associations for publishing magazines, scientific or professional journals, technical manuals, periodicals, newspapers, books, newsletters, brochures, reports, pamphlets, audiovisual materials, or computer databases and information sources might make defamatory statements themselves or permit others to do so. In fact, anyone who makes an oral or written communication concerning an identifiable individual, entity, product, or service can potentially commit defamation. Defamation could therefore be readily committed by those acting on behalf of an association as volunteers or employees and engaged in disciplinary or investigatory processes such as ethics enforcement, standards and certification for products or professionals, accreditation of graduate or continuing education, promulgating lists of credentialed providers of products or services, making personnel decisions, and so on.

What Are the Basic Principles of the Law of Defamation?

Defamation consists of the communication to a third party of a false, derogatory statement concerning a person, entity, product, or service, unless the communicator was privileged in making the communication.

Therefore, to give rise to liability:

1. A statement must be *about a particular, living individual or existing entity, or a product or service line of a particular entity*. The reference need not be by name; a statement may be defamatory if the listener or reader of the communication understands it to refer to a particular individual, entity, product, or service.
2. A statement must be *actually communicated to a third person* (in other words, to someone other than the speaker). Anyone who republishes (i.e., prints, reprints, repeats, paraphrases, or quotes, even with attribution) is equally responsible with the original speaker.
3. A statement must be *derogatory or damaging to the person's, entity's, product's, or service's reputation*. Accusing someone of dishonesty or other moral deficiency, or of professional or business deficiency, raises particularly significant risks of liability for defamation. *Any* derogatory statement of fact or implied fact may be defamatory, however.
4. A statement must be *false or misleading*. Truth is an absolute defense to virtually any defamation claim. Generally, the challenger, complainant, or plaintiff (the person about whom the statement was made) bears the burden of proving that the statement was false, at least where the statement is about a "matter of public concern."
5. A statement must not be protected by *privilege*:
    a. In many or most states, if a speaker takes reasonable precautions to ensure accuracy in every derogatory detail, including making reasonable inquiry, the speaker will not be held liable for defamation, even if the speech turns out to be false and defamatory.
    b. Where the statement concerns a public official or "public figure," the speaker will not be held liable unless the speaker actually knew that the accusations were false or made the statement in "reckless disregard" of its truth or falsity.
    c. Publication or communication of a derogatory statement within an association, including to members, for the purpose of promoting a common interest, may be protected by a "qualified privilege." For example, communications among members of an association's governing board regarding actual board business, or deliberations in the context of legitimate enforcement of a business or professional code, are likely to be protected by this "common interest" privilege. Employment recommendations or evaluations, made within or outside the association, enjoy a similar qualified privilege in most states. Where the privilege applies, these statements may give rise to liability only if motivated by spite or ill-will, or if communicated to persons beyond the management group or "need to know" circle.

True but *misleading* derogatory statements about persons, entities, products, or services may as fully generate liability as statements that are outright false.

Note that defamation may also occur in the employer–employee context, particularly where employment references are concerned. For this, and any other questions relating to human resources issues, see chapters 19 and 20 of this book.

Hypothetical Defamation Scenarios

The following scenarios do not refer to actual persons or organizations; their purpose is solely to illustrate the nature of risk faced from defamation actions by associations and their volunteers and employees.

Example 1: Publications

An association's scientific journal publishes an article by a professor (Member 1) at Major State University (MSU). Shortly after publication, the association receives a letter from another MSU faculty member (Member 2). Member 2 claims Member 1's article was substantially plagiarized from Member 2's own recently published work in an obscure journal. Member 2 demands that the association so state in the next issue of the same journal and threatens that if the association does not do so, Member 2 will sue the association for copyright infringement. Very upset by the allegations and risk of liability for infringement, facing an imminent publication deadline, and angered at the apparently unscrupulous conduct of Member 1, the association's journal editorial staff compares publication dates, ascertains that Member 2's substantially similar article was in fact published first, and in its next issue states that Member 1's article had been plagiarized.

Member 1 files a defamation action against the association, and the complaint names all association personnel responsible for the retraction as additional defendants. Member 1 testifies that although published second, the piece was actually written first and was pirated by Member 2. The jury finds that the association's characterization of the article as plagiarized was false and that the association was negligent in failing to ascertain the facts. It enters judgment jointly against the association and its individual employee defendants for a substantial award.

Example 2: Publications

This scenario is the same as Example 1, except that the association's employees do not react immediately to Member 2's charge of plagiarism. Instead, they consult the association's legal counsel and, under counsel's direction, directly contact Member 1, who is unable to explain the striking similarity of the articles. The association's editorial staff does everything they can think of to confirm or deny the plagiarism charge, short of informing any third parties not aware of the charges about them. They then publish a carefully worded statement, screened by counsel, that sets forth the facts as understood by them.

When Member 1 sues, and testifies as to authorship of the article first, the jury believes the testimony. Thus, it declares that the accusation of plagiarism was false. It enters judgment in favor of the association and the individual defendants anyway, however, because the association had not been negligent. It had instead taken all reasonable steps to ensure the accuracy of its report.

Example 3: Newsletters

A respected member of a statewide trade association of automobile service companies writes a letter to the editor of the association's newsletter. The letter says that a particular national chain of drive-in auto service firms that has recently begun doing business in the state is consistently employing untrained service professionals. The letter states the writer's opinion that the practice could result in severe safety hazards to motorists. The newsletter reprints the letter.

The chain sues the association, its newsletter staff, and the editorial review committee of volunteers for publishing the letter. The association argues that the letter contained only opinions, not facts, but the court rules otherwise. It finds that the letter to the editor implied the defamatory fact that the automobile service provided by the national chain was substandard and dangerous to motorists. It finds this implied statement of fact to be false, and that the association took no steps to verify its truth or falsity prior to printing the letter. It finds that the chain lost a significant number of customers as a result of the newsletter and awards a substantial sum as damages against the association and the individuals.

The simplest way for the association to have avoided this liability would have been to refrain from publishing the letter. If publishing the letter were important to the association, however, the newsletter staff should have contacted legal counsel *before* publishing the letter, in an attempt to find the means to minimize the association's legal risk (as well as the legal risk to the employees themselves and to the volunteers who performed editorial review for the newsletter). Legal counsel might have suggested that the association require the member to supply credible evidence that the auto service of the chain was substandard (and to ask the chain to respond to that evidence before publishing the letter). Only if the claims appeared to be accurate after a conscientious investigation should they have been published. Alternatively, legal counsel might have suggested that the member be asked to resubmit the letter in a different form—for example, without identifying the offending chain expressly or by implication, and/or without implying that the service provided was substandard.

Example 4: Accreditation

An educational program located in the State of New Amsterdam offers continuing education courses for specialty-practice health care professionals. The educational program applies for accreditation by a national association of health care professionals engaged in accreditation in this area. The association receives an anonymous letter stating that the applicant educational program routinely fails to provide refunds on a timely basis and grossly overcharges for course materials. The association makes appropriate inquiry of the program, which vigorously disputes the charges but also fails to provide definitive evidence refuting them. Lacking proof, and otherwise satisfied with the program, the association grants accreditation to the program. Subsequently, an employee of the association's accreditation department gives a speech at an association convention in New Amsterdam. The employee is asked a question concerning how the association's department deals with unsubstantiated allegations concerning programs being considered for accreditation. Without identifying the program by name, the employee relates the story of "a New Amsterdam program" that allegedly withheld refunds and overcharged for materials but that was accredited anyway in the absence of proof.

The educational program sues the association and the employee, claiming that the audience correctly identified the program, resulting in serious damage to its business. The court finds the association and the individual employee liable for a substantial amount in damages.

Liability of this nature can be avoided simply by avoiding "examples" based upon actual cases—or by changing the facts, details, and identifying information sufficiently so that *no one* could identify the hypothetical example with any particular program or person. It is wise to state expressly that one is stating a hypothetical example, not based upon any actual case. And when in doubt, answer generally without providing an example at all.

How Does One Minimize Risk to the Association and to Individuals From Defamation?

As suggested by the foregoing examples, any prospective publication or other communication that explicitly or implicitly concerns a particular individual, entity, product, or service raises a potential defamation issue. Whenever the publication or communication has a derogatory meaning, the following steps should be taken *before* issuing the publication or making the communication:

1. Determine whether the statement can simply not be made.
2. Determine whether it is possible to convey the essential information without the derogatory meaning.
3. If derogatory meaning must be conveyed, determine whether it is necessary to identify the individual, entity, product, or service concerned, either implicitly or explicitly. Is it possible to create a hypothetical formulation that will convey the same information without reflecting explicitly or implicitly on any real person or entity? Great care should be taken to ensure that hypotheticals do not imply facts about actual people, entities, and so on.
4. If derogatory information about a particular, identified or identifiable, subject must be conveyed, ensure that the audience for the communication is as small as possible while remaining consistent with the goals of the communication. If the communication can be limited to

the subject in question, this will minimize or eliminate the risk of legal exposure. Restricting the communication to association volunteers and employees sharing a common interest in its subject matter also may somewhat reduce risk.

5. Take all reasonable steps to ensure that every detail of the derogatory information related about an identified or identifiable person, entity, product, or service is true and not misleading. Contact the subject directly where reasonably possible. Insist on multiple independent sources, and create a paper record concerning those sources.

6. Information provided by persons with a reason to have personal animosity or ill will toward a subject—or with other reasons (e.g., economic) to wish the subject ill fortune—should be viewed with particular suspicion. Furthermore, individuals within an association who have or might appear to have such feelings toward the subject should not be put in a position to speak about the subject on the association's behalf or to supervise the speech of others concerning the subject.

7. *Most important*, before publishing or releasing a derogatory statement concerning an identified or identifiable person, entity, product, or service, ask legal counsel to review the document, the support for the statements made, and the need to make the statement at all or in its present form.

Part II

Legal Issues in Self-Regulation

Introduction

The chapters in Part II address legal issues that in some sense "regulate" the businesses or professions represented by associations. Standards, certification, accreditation, and mediation are examples of formal programs of association-conducted "self-regulation" of businesses or professions. However, any effort by an association to set criteria, principles, or standards, or to approve, endorse, or accredit individuals or entities, raises legal issues even more serious than those raised by formal self-regulation programs. Even restrictions on association membership are in this sense self-regulation. Thus, volunteers or employees of associations who are aware of, or are contemplating, self-regulatory activity for the association should consult the appropriate chapters in this part of the book.

Chapter 7 concerns "advice" or endorsements made by an association; chapter 8 concerns promulgation or enforcement of business or professional ethics codes; chapter 9 concerns promulgation or enforcement of accreditation or approval standards for educational or other programs outside the association; chapter 10 concerns issuance by associations of guidelines, advisories, models, or recommendations to members or others; chapter 11 concerns association activities in which credentials, or lists of qualified individuals or entities, are issued in particular fields of endeavor; chapter 12 concerns product standards, testing, and certification; and chapter 13 concerns association membership requirements.

7

Advice and Endorsements

What Are the Legal Risks to Associations From Advice and Endorsements?

Trade and professional associations typically have numerous publications and sponsor many educational programs in which statements might be made regarding the safety, efficacy, propriety, or other aspects of products, services, individuals, or entities that could be considered "advice." Usually the statements are attributed to authors, speakers, or others who are independent of the association, and in those cases, readers or listeners understand clearly that the statements are not those of the association. When a statement is not likely to be understood as carrying the official approval of the association for a product, service, individual, or entity, there is likewise little chance that the association could be successfully accused of responsibility for damages or injuries that result from reliance upon the statement.

By comparison, there are situations in which an association may reasonably be regarded as giving its official advice or providing its official endorsement, whether explicitly or implicitly, on issues of safety, efficacy, propriety, or other aspects of a product, service, individual, or entity in the field represented by the association. There is an increasing phenomenon of claims against associations for personal injuries or property damage allegedly resulting from reliance upon the associations' advice or endorsements. So far, the majority of these claims have ultimately failed. The few that have succeeded, however, merit close attention. There is certainly some legal risk for an association in connection with advice or endorsements. It should be understood clearly and managed carefully.

Who Is at Risk?

Any volunteer or employee of an association that commits, or appears to commit, the association to particular advice or endorsements may cause the association to incur liability based upon that advice or those endorsements.

What Legal Principles Govern Advice and Endorsements?

Two kinds of claims might be made against an association:

1. **Advice on matters of safety.** Here, the risk could be termed "derivative malpractice" or "derivative product liability." Conceptually, the

claim would be that an association has issued some guidelines, standards, or directions that arguably proved to be not only inaccurate but also harmful. According to the claimant, reliance on them resulted in injury or damage. Such a claim might be made by a member of the association or by a customer/patient/client of the member (see chap. 10, "Guidelines, Advisories, Models, or Recommendations").

2. **Direct or implied endorsements.** Here, the risk is endorsement liability. By "standing behind" or allowing its name and reputation to be used in connection with the promotion of a product, service, individual, or entity, the argument would be that an association effectively guaranteed that it would assume financial responsibility if the product, service, or entity proved to be harmful or ineffective. Note that this discussion concerns advice or endorsements that are *favorable* but are claimed to be inaccurate and damaging; contrast this with the situation in which associations' communications are unfavorable to individuals or entities. (See chap. 6, "Defamation.")

There are three basic elements necessary to hold associations responsible for injuries or damages relating to advice that they give or to endorsements that they make:

1. **Existence of a duty.** When faced with a claim that someone was personally injured or had property damaged because of advice offered by an association or because of dealing with a product, service, individual, or entity endorsed by an association, a court is likely to consider first whether the association owed a *duty* to the claimant. Resolution of that question will often depend on the extent to which the association officially participated in, or approved, the guidelines, standards, or directions—the "advice"—at issue. For endorsements, there would be an inquiry into whether the association had any control over the quality of the product, service, individual, or entity that it "stood behind." Even when it does not seem that the association intended to be responsible for advice given by others or endorsements of the products or services of others, the association could be found to have assumed that responsibility, such as through helping to determine what advice would be given or through testing the products or services endorsed. (See chap. 12, "Product Standards, Testing, and Certification.")

2. **Reliance by the claimant.** An equally critical consideration in a claim against an association in the area of advice or endorsements is whether the claimant actually *relied on* the association. It is ordinarily not sufficient, in attempting to bind the association to liability, for the claimant merely to show that the association gave advice or made an endorsement and that later an injury or damage occurred. It is crucial that the claimant be able to show that it was because of the

association's involvement that the advice was followed or the endorsed product or service was used.

3. **Negligence and causation.** Even in cases in which the court can find that the association owed a duty to the claimant and the claimant relied on the association, ordinarily the court will require something more before holding the association responsible for the injury or damage alleged. In most cases in this area so far, courts have felt the need to find that the association was *negligent* and that its negligence *caused* the injury or damage. Thus, there has been no "strict liability" theory imposed upon association advice or endorsements. The association must do something wrong, such as giving advice without adequate basis or endorsing services without checking references, and the claimant's injury must actually result from the association's wrongdoing.

Advice and endorsement liability may be best understood in the context of hypothetical association endeavors.

Hypothetical Scenarios Concerning Advice and Endorsements

The following scenarios are entirely fictional. They are designed to illustrate the nature of legal risks faced by associations, as well as their volunteers and employees, from providing advice or endorsements. Any resemblance to actual persons or entities is completely unintentional.

Example 1: Guidelines

An association of scientific researchers in human pathology determines that it will issue criteria to assist members in assessing the suitability of candidates to serve as human subjects in an area of the members' research. The candidate criteria are derived from several papers presented on the matter at association meetings or published in association journals, all by well-respected researchers and all following peer review. Later, a subject in a research study claims to have suffered personal injury as a result of participation in the study; the subject sues the researcher who conducted the study as well as the institution at which it was conducted. Those defendants in turn sue the association on the basis that they relied on its candidate criteria in selecting this subject for the research. One criterion in particular, when promulgated by the association, was missing an important qualification that would have excluded this subject from the research. The qualification appeared in the original paper from which the association derived the criteria, but the qualification was apparently inadvertently left out when the criteria were adopted and published by the association.

The association loses the suit. The court finds that the association clearly had a duty to the researchers for whom it promulgated the candidate selection criteria. It concludes that the member researcher relied upon the association's criteria, and it finds that the association was negligent in omitting an important qualification from the criteria that resulted directly in the inappropriate selection of the candidate. The association is ordered to reimburse the member researcher and the institution for their damages, as well as for their legal expenses and court costs.

Example 2: Endorsements

A trade association of firms in the securities industry is frequently asked by members to provide information about consultants who assist these kinds of businesses in data processing management. The association decides to conduct surveys and other research to identify and categorize data processing management consultants according to established standards (regional or national availability, minimum experience in the field, client satisfaction determined in objective sampling, etc.). A list of all identified consultants is published by the association, with special recognition given to those who achieved the highest level of ratings in the association's study.

One data processing management consulting firm, Elixir, Inc., achieved the association's highest rating and secures several engagements among members of the association, in part by referencing the association's rating. Elixir specializes in accounts receivable and consumer credit; it offers software and procedures for "dunning" overdue consumer accounts. After a period of time, the principal in Elixir dies and the firm dissolves; all of the firm's clients are investigated by the federal government and threatened with suit for having violated federal regulations on collection of consumer accounts. It develops that Elixir's software program was seriously deficient in not respecting the requirements of the law. All of the clients ultimately settle with the government, usually for substantial penalties. Together, they sue the association based upon the high rating that it had given to the now-defunct Elixir firm and seek substantial damages.

After legal proceedings lasting 3 years, the association is exonerated. The court finds that its surveying and researching of consulting firms was objective and appropriate. Although the association had a duty to its members, and the members relied upon the association's rating of the consultants, the association was not negligent in giving Elixir its highest rating. No damages are awarded against the association, but each side is required to pay its own legal expenses, which in the association's case are substantial.

How Does One Minimize Risk to the Association and Its Leadership?

There is a growing risk to associations from claims that injury or damage has been caused by association advice or endorsements. The following principles can help reduce that risk:

1. Associations should clearly recognize instances in which they can be perceived as providing "advice" or endorsements, especially as to safety,

efficacy, propriety, or other aspects of products, services, individuals, or entities.

2. All association guidelines, standards, directions, endorsements, or approvals should be carefully researched for substantive accuracy and reviewed for legal appropriateness before they are promulgated.

3. Associations should be very cautious in selecting "vendors" of endorsed products or services that the vendors are permitted to offer to the associations' members.

4. Associations should refrain as much as is feasible from involvement in, or control of, the products or services of outside vendors that the associations endorse.

5. When communicating to members the association's endorsement of products or services, care should be taken to avoid giving the impression that the association is guarantying the products or services.

6. Disclaimers may be useful in limiting associations' liability arising from both advice and endorsements.

8

Business and Professional Ethics

What Are the Legal Risks in Regulating Members' Ethics?

Many associations formulate and enforce codes of business or professional ethics or conduct. Ethics codes of associations often set forth both desirable goals and behavioral requirements considered essential for the protection of the public and for the optimal development of the businesses or professions represented by the associations. Enforcement ordinarily occurs according to a detailed set of procedures intended to ensure objectivity and fairness.

Both the establishment of ethical requirements and their enforcement are legally sensitive areas. For this reason, ethics enforcement should be entrusted solely to a discreet group within an association, either its governing board or a delegated committee, operating with the close assistance of the association's legal counsel. Ethics enforcement raises three primary kinds of legal risks:

1. **Antitrust issues.** Because ethical principles represent the consensus of an association's members regarding appropriate and fair business or professional conduct, and because violation of the principles may entail certain limited forms of collectively imposed sanctions, they are subject to federal and state antitrust laws prohibiting "contracts, combinations and conspiracies in restraint of trade." Ethics enforcement by associations has often been the subject of antitrust challenges when it was perceived as the effort of a group of competitors—the association membership or leadership—to unreasonably restrain competition, such as by raising, lowering, or stabilizing prices or fees; limiting nondeceptive advertising or promotion, scope of practice, or entry into markets; or boycotting suppliers, competitors, or customers/patients/clients. (See chap. 5, "Antitrust Generally.")
2. **Fairness issues.** In many states, when association-imposed discipline has adverse consequences for the member being disciplined, state law requires that such discipline be imposed only pursuant to "fair procedures" (i.e., procedures having the earmarks of "due process of law"). What "process" is "due" may vary from state to state and may vary depending on the form of discipline imposed.
3. **Defamation and confidentiality issues.** See chapters 6, "Defamation," and 2, "Respecting Confidentiality."

Who Is at Risk?

An association's development, promulgation, and enforcement of a code of business or professional ethics or conduct should be through a designated body within the association, and the process should be strictly committed to extensive procedural safeguards embodied in the governing documents of the association, ordinarily its bylaws or other rules established for the code authority within the association. *No other entity within an association—no board, task force, division, or committee—should develop, promulgate, or enforce ethical requirements.* The legal risks associated with any setting or enforcing of ethical rules other than through a process in the association's governing documents would be enormous and must be entirely avoided.

Of course, liability may also be incurred by volunteers or executives carrying out the code enforcement process sanctioned by the association's bylaws, if those individuals act improperly—such as by acting with improper motives or failing to follow established procedures. It is critical that persons involved in the enforcement of an association's business or professional code process comply with all applicable procedures and strictly observe conflict of interest rules. (See chap. 1, "Loyalty and Conflicts of Interest.")

What Legal Principles Govern Ethics Enforcement?

1. **Antitrust law.** *Any* action taken by an association that is viewed by a court as "anticompetitive" may violate the federal or state antitrust laws. Actions are anticompetitive when they raise prices or fees, restrict the supply of products or services, or lower the quality of products or services. Some kinds of actions are so likely to be anticompetitive that they should be avoided entirely, such as:
   a. provisions or procedures setting or suggesting maximum or minimum prices or fees to be charged or paid, or otherwise imposing upon the freedom of businesses or professionals to freely and individually establish prices or fees for their own products or services;
   b. provisions or procedures limiting or discouraging nondeceptive advertising of products or services; and
   c. provisions or procedures requiring or suggesting boycotts of suppliers, competitors, or customers/patients/clients.

   Many ethical rules are procompetitive—they result in better products or services, increased availability or access, or lower prices or fees. All ethical rules, however, must be evaluated to ensure that the motives and effects of the rule are to benefit competition in the ways deemed appropriate by the antitrust laws.

2. **Fairness requirements.** Associations can impose discipline, of course, only upon their members. In doing so, most important is the careful establishment and observance of rules and procedures to assure "due process" for members. The law requires due process, which means procedures that afford:
   a. written notice outlining the alleged violation, possible sanctions, and right to respond;
   b. opportunity to respond to the allegations of unethical conduct and to review and respond to all charges and evidence to be considered by the decision maker;

c. with respect to the most serious sanctions, the right to appeal an adverse decision to an unbiased decision-making body such as a board of directors, other governing body, or specially constituted, objective appeals board. (See chap. 1, "Loyalty and Conflicts of Interest.")

Hypothetical Ethics Enforcement Scenarios

The following scenarios are purely fictional. They are designed to exemplify the nature of legal risks from business or professional ethics enforcement faced by associations and their volunteers and executives from certain forms of legal action. Any resemblance to real persons or entities is unintentional.

Example 1: Divisions

A division of a state manufacturers' association is concerned about the importation of low-quality, foreign-made products by some competitors. It decides to promulgate a code of conduct applicable to division members that sets manufacturing standards and marketing guidelines. The division enforces the code with censure or expulsion from the division. The first member company expelled under the new code sues the leadership of the division and the association, arguing that the division's code process was unauthorized by the association's bylaws and deprived the member of rights to due process and fair procedure. The member company also argues that it did not commit the violation charged and that the action expelling it from the division has injured its reputation. The jury awards substantial damages.

Divisions, committees, or other units of associations must not establish nor enforce their own "codes of conduct" without clear authorization from the governing body of the association pursuant to the association's governing documents.

Example 2: Maximum Fees

The House of Delegates of a major national professional association, based upon the recommendation of a committee, determines that the charging of excessive fees by certain practitioners in the profession is gouging the public and damaging the good reputation of the profession. Accordingly, the House adds a provision to the association's ethics code rendering it unethical for a member to charge a fee for professional services that is higher than 25% above the average fee for comparable services in the member's community. A practitioner who objects to the provision, but has not been sanctioned under it, brings an antitrust suit against the association. The court enters an injunction and orders the association to pay the practitioner's lawyers the substantial costs of mounting the suit.

This sort of major liability risk is best prevented by avoiding entirely any pronouncements about prices or fees in the course of an association's promulgation and enforcement of ethical rules.

Example 3: Advertising About Fees

The same professional association's House of Delegates identifies another problem in the competitive marketplace. It decides that advertisements by certain practitioners—typically those very new to the profession or those who have recently immigrated from foreign countries—of extremely low fees for their professional services is disrupting established relationships among professionals who charge "market rate" fees. There are numerous demonstrated instances of consumers of the professional services choosing practitioners based upon low fees alone, resulting in their extreme dissatisfaction from low-quality services. The House concludes that the result is harm to the public, as well as harm to the profession. Without in any way restricting the fees actually charged and without banning advertising altogether, the House adds a provision to the association's ethics code banning the advertising of fees for professional services in the field represented by the association. An antitrust action is brought by several members to challenge the new provision. The association loses the action and is ordered to pay substantial damages, as well as the plaintiffs' attorney's fees and litigation expenses.

The prohibition on restricting fees extends to restrictions on advertising about fees. An association is free to prohibit advertising that is misleading, false, or deceptive, whether the advertising is about fees or any other subject. However, an association cannot prohibit, limit, or otherwise restrict truthful, nondeceptive advertising.

Example 4: Boycotts

The governing board of a chamber of commerce concludes that the chamber's business code does not have a sufficient deterrent effect on improper or unethical business behavior—false advertising, inadequate consumer redress, shoddy products or services, and so on. For that reason, the board of the chamber adds a provision to the business code banning any member from referring business to another member or former member that has received a public reprimand or has been expelled from the chamber for code violations. There is an ensuing class action antitrust suit filed by chamber members and former members that claim to have lost business as a result of the change in the code. Although the plaintiffs are unable to identify specific instances of lost business, they prevail in the suit based on the theory of the "chilling effect" of the code change.

Associations must leave the economic and other consequences of business and ethical discipline up to the marketplace. Associations are free to inform members and the public about the code transgressions, but it must leave to the marketplace the choice about what to do with that information.

Example 5: Ex Parte Contacts

One volunteer on a medical association's education committee has personal knowledge that a physician, Dr. X, who is a member of the association, has committed an extreme and blatant ethical violation resulting in serious injury to Dr. X's patient. The volunteer informs the education committee, and some members of that committee contact the patient. The patient tells committee members that he filed a complaint about Dr. X with the medical association's ethics committee but that the committee took no action. The education committee authorizes its chair to contact all ethics committee members to provide them with the personal information known to the education committee about Dr. X. The ethics committee takes up the matter with legal counsel, who advises the ethics committee that it must dismiss Dr. X's case due to the improper ex parte contacts (i.e., without notice to, or an opportunity given to contest the information by, the party adversely affected) from the education committee.

Any member of an association who has information about a business or professional code violation by another member should contact directly the association staff office that handles code matters and communicate that information only in the manner instructed by the staff there. Contacts with code committee volunteers or employees about specific cases are improper and could result in liability to the association or, as in this case, could at least disable the association from taking disciplinary action that would otherwise be appropriate and in the public interest.

Example 6: Biased Hearing Committee Member

An association's ethics procedures, set out in the association's bylaws, afford a hearing in most cases in which the ethics committee has recommended that a member be dropped from membership in the association as a result of an ethics violation. The panelists who rule in the hearing are selected by the president of the association. In one case, a panelist knows the complaining party but fails to reveal this relationship when asked by the ethics committee staff about any possible conflicts or relationships. The panel recommends that the member be dropped from membership, and the association's governing board upholds that recommendation. The member sues to challenge the action and discovers, in the course of the suit, that one panelist was biased. Both the panelist and the association are held liable for substantial damages.

This sort of liability based upon bias could be incurred at any stage of business or professional code enforcement proceedings. It can easily be avoided, however, if all participants disclose any knowledge they may have about a particular case, including knowledge about the complainant or complainee in the case, prior to taking part in it. Those who have knowledge should not participate in a case without the express approval of legal counsel after full disclosure of the circumstances. Regarding conflicts, also review chapter 1, "Loyalty and Conflicts of Interest."

How Does One Minimize Risk to Oneself and to the Association?

1. All provisions on business or professional conduct of members, whether or not enforceable, should be promulgated only as provided in the association's bylaws or other governing documents. Business or professional conduct provisions must be clearly stated in the code before they can be enforced. They may be enforced only as provided in the bylaws or other governing documents.
2. The procedures for development, promulgation, and enforcement of a business or professional code must be scrupulously followed by all participants in the code process.
3. Ex parte communications (those occurring at times and places other than in the actual code proceedings) with association volunteers responsible for code enforcement or review of code activities about any particular code matter should be strictly avoided. Communications about cases should only be made through the association staff responsible for the code program.
4. Full disclosure of any factor that might be considered bias or conflict of interest is essential, with recusal in appropriate cases.

9

Accreditation and Approval

What Are the Legal Risks From a Program of Accreditation or Approval?

Trade and professional associations alike are increasingly engaging in programs of accreditation or approval of members' educational institutions, manufacturing or service facilities, or other training or business operations. The accrediting or approval functions of an association are intended to benefit the general public, prospective users/students/customers/patients/clients, and the profession or industry itself. As with other "self-regulation" programs of associations, it is crucial that each accrediting or approval program be conducted using reasonable criteria and following strict procedures to ensure that legal risks are minimized.

In the educational setting, courts have consistently recognized that accreditation of institutions and instructional programs serves useful educational and professional goals. Indeed, courts have noted that the restrictions on access by imposition of educational and training requirements are definitional aspects of the term *profession*. Courts have also granted that promulgation of accreditation criteria, and information concerning which institutions satisfy those criteria, is protected to a significant degree by the First Amendment to the U.S. Constitution. The First Amendment also provides at least limited protection for lobbying efforts designed to obtain official recognition for accreditation criteria or for the accreditation or approval decisions of associations. Although association-sponsored accreditation in the educational context has a longer history than association-sponsored accreditation or approval in other contexts, such as health care facilities or business service operations, nevertheless, the legal precedents and principles already established for academic accreditation can be expected to be applied elsewhere when opportunities arise.

Accreditation and approval activities of associations generally entail three kinds of legal risk:

1. **Antitrust issues.** (See chap. 5, "Antitrust Generally.") Unsuccessful applicants for accreditation or approval, or students or other users of unaccredited or unapproved programs, may seek to use the antitrust laws to obtain accreditation or approval, or damages for the program's failure to be accredited or approved. An association could be held liable under those laws if the challenger can demonstrate that accreditation or approval is very important to economic success and that the program's exclusion was the result of unreasonable or invalid criteria or of unfair or inappropriate procedures. As with all antitrust actions,

the key factor in an antitrust challenge to an association's accreditation or approval process is whether the association's actions are "anticompetitive" within the meaning of the antitrust laws. In short, did those actions have the effect of raising, lowering, or stabilizing prices (e.g., tuition or other costs of education or prices or fees at noneducational facilities) or of reducing the quantity or quality of products or services available?

2. **Fairness issues.** State common law can be invoked to require that private accreditation or approval be fair. Accreditation or approval criteria and exclusions are evaluated on a case-by-case basis. They are deemed invalid when they are unreasonable, arbitrary, or unsupported by the evidence. They may also be set aside if inadequate procedures are employed or if the established procedures of the accrediting or approval body are not followed in a particular case.

3. **Defamation issues.** See chapter 6, "Defamation."

Who Is at Risk?

As with ethics enforcement and other "self-regulation" by associations, accreditation or approval must be conducted consistent with authority granted in the association's bylaws or other governing documents. Ad hoc, informal, or "rump" approval programs or endeavors carry great potential risk and must be completely avoided.

Even for formally authorized programs, however, liability may be incurred by volunteers or employees carrying out the accreditation or approval processes within an association if those individuals act improperly—such as by acting with improper motives or failing to follow established procedures. It is critical that persons involved in those processes comply with all applicable procedures and strictly observe conflict of interest rules. (See chap. 1, "Loyalty and Conflicts of Interest.")

What Legal Principles Govern Accreditation and Approval?

1. **Antitrust law.** "Anticompetitive actions," as defined in the federal antitrust laws, are unlawful. (See chap. 5, "Antitrust Generally.") Accreditation and approval criteria must not have the purpose or primary effect of raising, lowering, or stabilizing prices or fees, restricting the supply of products or services, or lowering the quality of products or services. Accreditation and approval criteria should be objectively grounded—that is, based on data or on a respected body of professional, educational, or business opinion developed by recognized experts and linking each particular criterion to more successful achievement of valid quality goals. It is critical to the legality of accreditation and approval criteria that commercial and economic considerations play no role whatsoever in setting or applying them.

2. **Fairness requirements.** Most important is careful establishment and strict observance of rules and procedures for the accrediting or approval program. The law requires that criteria be neither excessively vague nor unduly rigid. Procedures generally must afford the applicant written notice of adverse decisions, stating the reasons for the failure to accredit or approve, placement on probation, or other adverse decision; they must afford the applicant an adequate opportunity to respond to the reasons stated as supporting the adverse decision; and they must afford applicants denied accreditation or approval, or otherwise receiving an adverse determination, such as probation, an appeal to an impartial tribunal. It is also critical that conflicts of interest be strictly avoided by members of association accrediting bodies and appeal panels. (See chap. 1, "Loyalty and Conflicts of Interest," regarding conflicts of interest issues.)

Hypothetical Scenarios Concerning Accreditation and Approval

The following scenarios are fictional. They are designed solely to illustrate the nature of legal risks faced by associations, as well as their volunteers and employees, from certain forms of legal action in connection with accreditation and approval programs.

Example 1: Minimum Tuition Criterion

A substantial group within the House of Delegates of a national professional association engaged in academic accreditation for postgraduate programs in the profession believes that several universities have set tuition at levels so low that it threatens the quality of education offered by those institutions. Arguing that monitoring the levels of tuition is simpler than quantifying the many ways in which low tuition can injure the quality of education, the delegates succeed in passing a "Sense of the House" resolution urging the association's Accreditation Board to review tuition levels in determining whether to grant accreditation. In debate on the floor of the House of Delegates, several delegates argue that "cut-rate tuition" is forcing even established programs to hold down tuition increases. The Accreditation Board collects tuition data in connection with its program reviews and denies accreditation to a program with low fees. That program challenges its exclusion under this criterion. The court finds against the association, holding that the Accreditation Board effectively applied a tuition minimum, which constitutes a per se violation of the antitrust laws. The association is held liable for a substantial judgment.

An association engaged in academic accreditation or other approval programs should strictly avoid criteria that set prices or violate any of the per se categories in the antitrust laws and should avoid political or other processes that attempt to exert *any* influence on fees or prices through an accrediting or approval function. (See chaps. 5, "Antitrust Generally," and 11, "Professional Specialization, Certification, Recognition, and Listing.")

Example 2: Criteria Unsupported by Data and Conflict of Interest

Several "innovative" educational programs in a profession deemphasize the use of standard textbooks in the field in favor of courses of self-directed readings worked out by student and professor. Concern arises within the national association responsible for accreditation of educational programs for the profession that these innovative programs are failing to "socialize" their students adequately into the professional community. Three prominent association members—who are themselves authors of principal texts in the field—work behind the scenes and persuade the association's governing body to amend the accreditation criteria to require that a certain number of "generally recognized" textbooks be assigned to every degree candidate by accredited programs. A class action is brought on behalf of all of the nontextbook programs, claiming that the new criterion is unsupported by data or by respected pedagogic opinion to the effect that the textbooks in question produce superior professionals. The lawsuit further charges that the central motivation for the criterion was economic. The court reviews the matter under the Rule of Reason and sides with the challenging programs. The court recognizes that considerable deference is owed to an expert body such as a national association when it sets educational criteria but cites the association's inability to offer any support for the socialization criterion in the literature. The court also expresses concern that major players within the association seeking the criterion change were motivated by economic self-interest. A substantial dollar judgment is entered against the association and the central figures in obtaining the changed criterion.

Before enacting any criterion change in an accreditation program, an association should conduct a careful review to ensure that the change is supportable if challenged in court. A wide array of opinions from the potentially affected community should be solicited, and criteria should be adopted only if data demonstrate that they lead, as a rule, to improved quality of education, or if there is a respected body of professional and academic opinion, that it will lead to an improvement in the quality of education. Persons with a direct financial stake in the adoption of particular criteria should be excluded from the process, or at any rate their bias should be disclosed, and the association should make certain that valid reasons, not a bias, lie behind the adoption of criteria.

Example 3: Inappropriate Pressure Outside the Approval Process

A health care association maintains an Internship Committee, which approves internship programs at specialty treatment facilities of hospitals on an institution-by-institution basis. According to the bylaws of the association, the Committee makes its approval decisions without bias and autonomously from other association bodies. Members of the association's governing board receive information reflecting sexual harassment of interns in Good Health Hospital's approved internship program. The board investigates, and it passes a resolution urging that the approval of the program be withdrawn by the Internship Committee. Numerous members of the association's governing board contact members of the Internship Committee by telephone and by letter. In those calls, the board representatives relate the facts as they know them and urge that the Committee take action. As it happens, the staff of the Internship Committee had received a formal complaint about the sexual harassment at the Good Health Hospital internship program at the very same time that the governing board had learned about it, and the Committee had already initiated an independent investigation. Upon learning about the contacts from board members, the staff of the Committee consults with legal counsel. Legal counsel advises the Internship Committee that the widespread ex parte contacts with Committee members raise the level of risk to the association to an unacceptable level. The Internship Committee is forced to drop inquiry into the complaint, and the program at Good Health Hospital retains its approval.

It is very important that contacts with the accreditation or approval program proceed only as mandated in the association's governing documents or other established rules and procedures. Where autonomy is granted to an accrediting or approval body, all other individuals and bodies of the association should refrain from attempting to influence the process.

Example 4: Following Procedures and Avoiding Evidence Obtained "Outside the Record"

Pro-Ed is a commercial firm that offers continuing education (CE) for human resources management professionals; it files an application for approval by a national association that approves these programs. The application is thorough and complete, and, from all appearances, Pro-Ed seems to be well run and adequately administered. The quality of its CE programs appears high. In the initial review of Pro-Ed's application by a subcommittee of the association's approval committee, the subcommittee judges Pro-Ed worthy of 2-year preliminary approval, signifying that Pro-Ed meets all established association criteria, and makes a formal, written recommendation of approval. During the course of discussion in the full approval committee, however, one committee member relates having attended one of Pro-Ed's CE courses several years earlier and finding the material presented to be "bizarre" and "inappropriate." Another committee member recounts that a relative had much the same experience in another CE course offered by Pro-Ed. Based on this information, the committee declines to accept the subcommittee's recommendation or to issue an approval to Pro-Ed, fearing that its quality was not as high as had appeared in the application. Unknown to the approval committee, Pro-Ed had stopped offering the two CE courses in question when it had received complaints similar to those voiced by committee members. Its remaining courses were not subject to those defects. Pro-Ed successfully sues the association, receiving a substantial award.

It is critical that applications for approval or accreditation be judged *solely* on the official record. If a member of a reviewing body is privy to information outside the record, the member should disclose that fact, and, if the information is such that the member cannot fairly judge the matter based upon the record, the member should be recused from the process.

Example 5: Conflicts of Interest

A utility company, Power, Inc., applies for approval of its nuclear power plant control room design and operation by a national association in which the utility holds membership. The association maintains an approval program for such facilities. The application is incomplete and it is evident to the association committee reviewing the application that the applicant, Power, Inc., does not understand the association's criteria and procedures for control room approval. The committee declines to recommend approval of the facility, citing Power, Inc.'s fundamental misunderstanding of the criteria and pointing out, in the committee's review report, the mistakes made on the application. Representatives of Power, Inc. consult the executive staff of the association for help in reapplying and ask for the names and telephone numbers of the members of the reviewing committee so that they may be contacted for clarification of points made in the report. Through this endeavor, Power, Inc. learns that one of the committee reviewers is a consultant who has, for many years, advised competing utilities regarding the design and operation of nuclear power plant control room design and operation. Power, Inc. writes to the association, charging that the reviewer has a conflict of interest.

Although confident that the reviewer's actions were not in fact improperly motivated, the association decides to have the committee reconsider the initial application, employing reviewers with no conceivable economic conflict of interest.

It is not obvious whether the utility, Power, Inc., would have a claim here. Plainly, however, the reviewer should have disclosed to the association and to the applicant the potential conflict and probably should have been recused from the process. It is also highly questionable whether the executive staff of the association should have "consulted" with a known applicant and provided identifying information on the committee reviewers.

How Does One Minimize Risk to the Association and to Individuals?

1. Only the specific bodies within an association designated in the governing documents as responsible for a particular accreditation or approval process should adjudicate or take a position with respect to accreditation or approval of specific applicants. No other board, committee, or other body in the association should exert pressure on the

accreditation or approval process regarding review of specific applicants.

2. The rules of the accreditation or approval process must be scrupulously followed by all participants.

3. Ex parte communications (those occurring at times and places other than in the actual accreditation or approval proceedings) with the relevant reviewing committee or board, site visitors, or hearing panelists about any particular application for which they have responsibility should be strictly avoided. Communications about pending applications should be handled through the association's executive staff responsible for assisting the accreditation or approval program.

4. Full disclosure of any factor that might be considered bias or conflict of interest is essential, with recusal in appropriate cases.

5. Accreditation or approval criteria should be adopted for valid reasons only, and commercial or economic motivations should be particularly shunned. Care should be taken to ensure that objective bases support each accreditation or approval criterion.

6. Accreditation or approval decisions should be based completely and exclusively on the "record" of the review, not on extraneous, anecdotal, subjective, or other outside sources of information.

10

Guidelines, Advisories, Models, or Recommendations

What Are the Legal Risks From Guidelines, Advisories, Models, or Recommendations?

Associations of all kinds and sizes often issue pronouncements to assist members in conducting their businesses or practicing their professions. Quite apart from product standards, testing, and certification that are so ubiquitous, particularly in manufacturing associations (see chap. 12 in this volume), many associations give advice to members on a less formal basis and on a broader range of subjects. Guidelines might be published for performing a particular procedure. Advisories might be issued to warn of safety hazards or emergency situations. Models might be offered with the suggestion that they be copied or modified by members. Recommendations could include communications, however labeled, that suggest a particular course of conduct. In addition, without labeling the communication a "guideline," "advisory," "model," or "recommendation," associations may issue communications that include explicit or implicit suggestions or directions to members. Guidelines, advisories, models, recommendations, and similar communications are distinguishable from product standards (see chap. 12) or business and professional ethics codes (see chap. 8) because they are not ostensibly subject to any *compulsion*, such as by industry practice, or *enforcement*, such as by an association's disciplinary system.

Association guidelines, advisories, models, and recommendations (grouped in this chapter and collectively called "guidelines"), even when issued without enforcement mechanisms, have been challenged under the antitrust laws, at times successfully, when they were alleged to have restrained competition unreasonably by directing, channeling, coercing, or otherwise influencing members toward anticompetitive conduct. When directive communications are supported by so prestigious an organization as an industry's or profession's association, there can be a "chilling effect" on the conduct of members, which is considered tantamount to an agreement among them on joint action. Even when the directives serve other legitimate ends, if they also restrain competition, such as through price or fee setting, market or customer allocation, or boycotting of suppliers or others, then the association may be seriously at risk of violating the antitrust laws. (See chap. 5, "Antitrust Generally.") Guidelines may also expose an association, as well as individual volunteers or employees, to liability for derivative malpractice or for endorsement liability. (See chap. 7, "Advice and Endorsements.")

Who Is at Risk?

Any association volunteer or employee may incur individual liability, and liability for the association as a whole, by establishing guidelines in improper ways. Because it is the *appearance* of the association's endorsement that can lead to liability, liability may be incurred even if the association has not formally approved the guidelines. (See chap. 3, "Apparent Authority.") Care should be taken, therefore, to ensure that even *proposals* for guidelines are clearly labeled as such and brought to the attention of senior association executives and legal counsel.

What Legal Principles Apply to Guidelines?

Association pronouncements, such as guidelines, advisories, models, or recommendations, that have a substantial purpose or effect of unreasonably limiting competition may be found in violation of the antitrust laws even when they are clearly promulgated as voluntary rather than mandatory. Purposes and effects most likely to violate the antitrust laws include raising or stabilizing prices or fees; allocating markets or customers; or boycotting suppliers, reimbursers, competitors, or others.

Naked attempts at price fixing, market allocation, or boycotting are likely to be deemed unlawful per se (i.e., in and of themselves). Otherwise, an association's guidelines, if subjected to an antitrust challenge, will be analyzed by the courts to determine if their effects on competition are "reasonable" in light of their purposes. The key question will be whether the guidelines, on balance, will raise prices or fees or lower the quality or quantity of available products or services (see chap. 5, "Antitrust Generally"). The courts will balance any adverse competitive effects (e.g., fewer endorsed service providers) against benefits to competition (e.g., increased quality of services or greater information about services in the hands of the public). Generally, any action likely to raise or stabilize prices or fees, or lower the quantity or quality of products or services, should be carefully weighed before it is taken. The courts are likely to ask whether

1. there are appropriate purposes for the guidelines not related to restraining competition (scientific study, product quality, etc.);
2. the guidelines actually advance purposes that are unrelated to restraining competition; and
3. the association, in developing the guidelines, has chosen the means to achieve its purposes that are likely to have the fewest adverse effects upon competition.

Guidelines can also raise defamation issues or product liability issues for associations. (See chaps. 6, "Defamation," and 7, "Advice and Endorsements.")

Hypothetical Scenarios Concerning Guidelines

The following scenarios are fictional. Their only purpose is to illustrate the nature of legal risks faced by association volunteers and employees.

Example 1: Reasonableness

A group of allied health professionals within a national association learns that an innovative methodology for conducting a certain type of research using human subjects, the Helix Protocol, is being employed in several locations without the extraordinary safeguards that the group considers appropriate for this research. There are potentially serious adverse results for the subjects. The group's leadership consults with recognized experts, considers alternatives, and concludes that the public and the profession would be best served if the association were to promulgate a warning regarding use of the Helix Protocol. After review by the association's legal counsel, the group issues a press release on behalf of the association and places articles in association publications recommending that the Helix Protocol methodology be used only with extraordinary additional safeguards for human subjects. The group calls for a voluntary moratorium by all members of the profession on use of the Helix Protocol unless they employ the extraordinary safeguards recommended. The safeguards are difficult and expensive to provide.

Several professionals disagree with the group's conclusions. They are all using the Helix Protocol in their scientific research and claim that they have found it to be safe without special safeguards for subjects. They sue the association to obtain an injunction requiring it to retract its communications on this issue. The plaintiffs and their organizations derive considerable research grant revenue from this aspect of their scientific endeavors, which they say has been jeopardized by the association's pronouncements. They claim that the activist group within the association had competitive motives for issuing the call for a moratorium.

The court rules in favor of the association. It notes that the association has a right, if not an obligation, to speak out in such situations. Although it recognizes the possibility that this controversy involves financial considerations, the court concludes that the association acted responsibly and in the public interest in making its determination regarding the matter and in issuing the call for a voluntary moratorium. Each party is required to bear its own legal fees and costs.

Example 2: Competitive Motives

Extensive media attention has been given to a form of therapy that relies entirely upon fasting to cure serious mental illnesses among adolescents. Many film and political personalities, whose children have undergone the therapy, endorse and recommend it to the public, even though no scientific research has been conducted regarding the safety and efficacy of the therapy and its

practitioners have no conventional education or training in psychology, nu-
trition, or medicine. At the urging of many members of a statewide mental
health professionals' association, the association launches a six-figure, mul-
tiyear campaign to stamp out this form of therapy as harmful to the public.

The association's campaign includes, among other endeavors

1. entreaties to private health care reimbursers urging that they refrain
    from paying for the therapy;
2. leaked stories to reporters transmitting the rumors that the endorsers
    were paid for their endorsements;
3. amendment of the association's ethical code to ban all patient referrals
    to, or any professional relationships with, individuals who have en-
    gaged in this form of therapy; and
4. amendment of the association's educational accreditation criteria to
    prohibit accredited programs from conducting research or education
    in the therapy.

The proponents of the fasting therapy for adolescents bring a lawsuit
against the state association, alleging that it has engaged in an antitrust
boycott.

After 3 years of pleadings, discovery, and trial proceedings, the court finds
against the association. It notes that the association's ends may have been
sound but that its means were illegal. The court avoids consideration of whether
there is adequate scientific basis for the fasting therapy but points to evidence
that some mental health professionals in the association's membership had
substantial competitive motives in urging the association's expansive campaign. It finds several aspects of the association's campaign to have been
excessive and unjustified. Substantial damages are assessed against the association, including an order that the association must retract its statements
about the therapy, "neutralize" those statements through other positive communications to members and the public, delete references to the therapy in
its ethics code and accreditation criteria, and refrain from making negative
comments about the therapy in the future.

How Does One Minimize Risk to the Association and to Individuals?

To fulfill its mission on behalf of members as well as on behalf of the public,
an association engages in extensive communications on all subjects related to
the business or the profession that it represents. At times, it may be in the
best interests of the association's constituencies or of the public for the association to promulgate communications in the form of guidelines, advisories,
models, or recommendations. In those situations, the following considerations
should apply:

1. There should always be important, compelling, and defensible bases for the association to issue communications in the form of guidelines, advisories, models, or recommendations. Some appropriate goals not adequately addressed by the government or by other organizations should be at stake. When there are acceptable alternatives to the use of association guidelines, such as educational publications or programming, they should be considered first.

2. In any antitrust challenge, the association's guidelines will be subjected to a review of their "reasonableness." Therefore, every effort should be made to assure and document that the premises and conclusions in such directives are well researched, based on broadly accepted principles, a respected body of expert opinion, or empirical data; consistent and moderate in their means and goals; and subjected to peer review by respected members of the business or profession and perhaps those in other disciplines whose input may help ensure reasonableness. Valid surveying of opinion in the field may be warranted.

3. It should be readily apparent that any association guidelines are intended to be voluntary. Although it is clear that even voluntary directives from an association have potential legal consequences, the ramifications of mandatory rules and regulations are more severe. If there is any possibility of confusion or misunderstanding regarding the voluntary nature of the association's pronouncements on guidelines, that fact should be stated prominently in any introduction to, or description of, the pronouncements.

4. A deliberate effort should be made in developing any association guidelines to identify and evaluate the potential effects on competition. Consideration should be given to whether the pronouncements might have effects upon (a) prices or fees for products or services; (b) populations or areas in which products or services will be offered; or (c) relationships with suppliers, competitors, or users of products or services.

   Where it is perceived that there could or will be effects on competition, every effort should be made to minimize any *adverse* effects (i.e., tendencies to raise or stabilize prices or fees, or reduce the quantity or quality of products or services available to the public). If an association were to issue guidelines applicable to a field of endeavor not ordinarily represented by the association, or one with which the association's members compete or might compete, special concerns would be raised about the effects upon competition.

5. Because of the serious legal ramifications of the issuance of guidelines, advisories, models, or recommendations by an association, these pronouncements should never be issued without complete legal review.

11

Professional Specialization, Certification, Recognition, and Listing

How Do Certification and Listing Programs Pose Legal Risks for Associations?

Many associations, particularly individual membership societies, have implemented specialization, certification, recognition, or listing programs to identify and publicize those who meet particular professional criteria. *Specialization* credentialing often has the practical or legal result of excluding noncredentialed professionals from practice within the specialty. *Certification* or *recognition*, in contrast, often denote that generalists have special qualifications in the credentialed area but may not restrict practice within that area by noncredentialed individuals. *Listing* programs may simply identify professionals who have obtained some credentials provided by other organizations or institutions. Professions in the health care field (e.g., medicine, nursing, dentistry) have long maintained specialty certification programs in various forms; listing programs are less common, although many such programs exist as well. Private professional certification, as distinguished from state governmental licensing, is ordinarily based on a candidate's ability to meet established criteria for postgraduate education, structured professional training, and passage of written or practical examinations. Recognition programs generally do not necessarily suggest employment qualifications but instead, the judgment of peers regarding professional commitment, achievement, service, and so on; they may or may not include examinations. Listing programs are often based on the presentation of credentials in education or professional references only, without separate examinations.

Professional specialization, certification, recognition, and listing programs can benefit the public. They assist lay persons in distinguishing professionals with special expertise or experience, establish baseline criteria that tend to elevate the levels of practice, and serve as references for third-party reimbursement mechanisms. The programs also can benefit the profession. They provide marks of distinction and recognition that can enhance prestige, tend to elevate the level of competence in a field, and can serve to increase professional earning power.

Professional specialization, certification, recognition, and listing programs (collectively termed *credentialing* here) are not without significant legal risk, however. They are inherently selective—some candidates or applicants achieve the desired credentials, whereas others do not. Those who are not successful may become antagonistic to the programs and mount legal challenges against them. The benefits of professional credentialing are substantial and are often well worth pursuing. However, caution and care must be exercised in developing and operating these credentialing programs because, if not carefully promulgated, they can become "lightning rods" for controversy.

Who Is at Risk?

Any association that issues or appears to issue credentials to individuals may be liable under any of the legal theories in the following discussion. There is also some risk that individuals, such as association volunteers or employees, could incur personal liability in connection with credentialing programs in some circumstances.

What Legal Principles Govern Credentialing Determinations?

There are two major types of legal risk to an association from credentialing programs:

1. **Antitrust.** As with denial of membership in an association, withholding of professional credentials may run afoul of the federal antitrust law against "contracts, combinations and conspiracies in restraint of trade." Where a program is created and run by an association consisting of professional "competitors" and the program confers benefits that are important to "competition" among the professionals, withholding of credentials on arbitrary or unreasonable grounds can be declared an illegal boycott. (See chap. 5, "Antitrust Generally.")
2. **Due process.** Even where an unsuccessful applicant or candidate for participation in a credentialing program fails to convince a court that the antitrust laws were violated, the denial of a credential may be defective on procedural grounds. Credentialing is a form of association self-regulation of professions. As such, it is required by law to afford fundamental due process to applicants and candidates. Before professional credentials can be withheld, those who seek the credentials should be provided at least (a) *notice* of the withholding of a credential and the reasons for it, (b) an *opportunity to respond* to the notice, and, at least in some states, (c) an *opportunity to appeal* to a body not involved in the original unfavorable decision. Rules must be applied consistently and impartially. There must be no actual or apparent bias by those responsible for the program (see chap. 1, "Loyalty and Conflicts of Interest"). Some states have additional requirements for due process by nongovernmental self-regulating bodies.

Credentialing programs may also raise legal concerns in other areas, such as defamation (see chap. 6), advice and endorsements (see chap. 7), and discrimination (see chap. 4). Federal law on accommodation for the disabled, the

Americans With Disabilities Act, specifically applies to private professional credentialing programs.

As a general rule, as credentialing programs become more "successful," they have increased risk of legal challenges and are subject to closer scrutiny by courts. A program that is developed and operated primarily for recognition of professional achievement, so long as it is perceived as such by the professionals and by the users of their professional services, will often be given greater deference and allowed more latitude by a reviewing court. By comparison, the more a credentialing program is intended or used for decisions on hiring or engagement, for assignment of professional tasks, or for reimbursement by third parties, the closer will be the legal scrutiny, with less latitude allowed. The following principles apply.

1. **Reasonable criteria.** The criteria selected in a credentialing program should be objectively grounded measures of professional competence for the level at which the program is aimed (entry level, achievement level, etc.). Criteria should be based on data or on a respected body of professional or educational opinion linking each particular criterion to the qualities that the credential purports to measure. Any reasonable combination of education, experience, and examination criteria is appropriate. Generally, criteria should not be unnecessarily stringent. The specification of alternative paths to certification or listing is desirable to increase access to the program. References by other professionals may be useful in corroborating information provided by applicants or candidates but should not be used for "blackballing."

2. **"Grandfathering."** A certification, listing, or other credentialing program may have difficulty at the time of start-up in attracting the participation of large numbers of professionals, especially where the program is to include written or practical examinations. It is therefore common to "grandfather" those who have extensive education and experience in a field for a limited period at the initiation of a program, thereby waiving the later examination requirement. Courts have consistently upheld the legality of grandfathering when it is done reasonably.

3. **Promotion.** Nothing prevents a professional credentialing program from publicizing information regarding participants in the program among users or reimbursers of professional services. However, care should be taken to avoid any explicit or implicit disparagement of nonparticipants (see chap. 6, "Defamation"), as well as any explicit or implicit endorsement or warranty of the services of the participating professionals (see chap. 7, "Advice and Endorsements").

Hypothetical Credentialing Scenarios

The following scenarios illustrate the legal risks and principles of professional credentialing programs that might be conducted by associations. Any resemblance to actual persons or existing entities is completely unintentional.

Example 1: Reasonableness

A division of a professional engineering specialty association is concerned that state-licensed engineers who lack training and experience in the specialty area are nevertheless routinely accepting employment or engagements in that area, leading to a reduced quality of services and a concomitant reduced regard by users of the services. The division decides to develop a program to confer a singular credential on engineers in the specialty area, based on three criteria: (a) membership in the division, (b) proof of at least 5 continuous years of full-time involvement in the area, and (c) nominations by at least five members of the division, including two members of the division board. The division intends that the specialty credentialing program would eventually be adopted by state licensing boards in engineering so that, when fully implemented by the states, only those who have been certified would be permitted to practice in the specialty.

A licensed engineer, X, who is a member of the association but not a member of this division, and who has written and lectured extensively in the area of engineering that is the subject of the division's program, applies for but is denied the specialty credential. X alleges that, since the division's program was developed, several consulting engagements have been lost in part because those offering the engagements required the division's specialty credential as one qualification. X notes the prospect of possible adoption of the specialty credentialing program by the state licensing board in the state. X brings an antitrust suit against the association, seeking an injunction barring the association's division from denying its specialty credential to X. The thrust of the suit is that the division, through its leadership, has effectively boycotted X from access to the credential and has illegally "tied" specialization to division membership, which X does not care to maintain. In its response, the association's division argues that X is also eligible for division membership, that division membership is a valid criterion for certification because of the publications and education offered by the division, and that the division took no steps to urge the use of its certification as a qualification for consulting assignments.

The court rules against the association. It orders the certification program to be reformulated to eliminate the membership requirement, and it seriously questions the validity of the requirement for five references. The court also awards damages and costs to the challenging engineer, X.

Example 2: Due Process

A committee of a national manufacturing association is asked by a governmental defense reimbursement agency to develop and maintain an annual listing of all individuals who are qualified to perform a particular kind of electronic maintenance service that is extensively reimbursed by the agency. The agency, through its electronic maintenance services advisory panel, recommends education and experience criteria that the panel considers minimally necessary for competence in this area. The association committee uses the association's publication channels to solicit applications from all individuals, whether their companies are association members or not, who would like to be listed. Those whose applications appear to meet the government's criteria are notified of their acceptances for the listing; the others are notified that they cannot be listed and are urged try again the following year.

One unsuccessful applicant, Z, challenges the decision. Z demands a full explanation as to why Z's qualifications were found insufficient. The committee declines to give details in order to protect the confidentiality of the process. Z sues. In discovery, Z learns that one of several committee members who reviewed Z's application was also Z's manager in a former employment position who had had an antagonistic relationship with Z and had threatened to have Z fired from the position. The record did not show whether that reviewer had recommended against acceptance of Z's application for listing by the committee.

The court rules in favor of Z. It finds that the appearance or possibility of bias and impartiality is sufficient to warrant overturning the denial of listing by the committee. It also questions the lack of notice of the reasons for the decision and the opportunity to respond. The court orders a new, objective review by the committee, republishing of the entire list if necessary, and an award of damages and costs to Z.

Example 3: Certification

A regional health care specialty association decides to develop a program of specialty certification in the area of its members' health care practice and to offer the program to state licensing boards in the region through contracts with the association. The association intends that, if the certification program were adopted by a state board, professionals who did not hold the specialty certification in that state could not legally practice in their field. The association is careful to establish reasonable and valid criteria and to use reasonable and fair procedures in the program. Nevertheless, the program is challenged by a group of the association's members who prefer to have "general" licenses in their field. The challengers allege antitrust, defamation, discrimination, and other violations of the law by the association in developing the program and offering it to state licensing boards.

The suit is dismissed by the court, which notes that specialization can serve useful and procompetitive functions when conducted properly. The court finds no substantive or procedural deficiencies in the association's program.

Example 4: Promotion

A state association of attorneys institutes a program offering voluntary specialty certification based upon education, experience, and examinations in several areas of the law. The program has extensive due process features and becomes recognized and respected. The association's office that manages the certification program learns that a large and dominant employer in the state, MegaCorp, which funds a legal reimbursement program for employees belonging to a union, the International Brotherhood of Brothers (IBB), is considering withdrawing reimbursement for all legal services in the next round of labor contract negotiations, in part out of concern for possible overuse of the program by covered employees. Representatives of the association's office meet with MegaCorp and with IBB; they provide convincing evidence that the overuse risk can be reduced by limiting reimbursement in the program to attorneys who are certified by the association. MegaCorp and IBB agree to the limitation and adopt it in their next collective bargaining agreement.

An investigation is brought by the Federal Trade Commission (FTC), followed by a complaint alleging that MegaCorp, IBB, and the association have entered into a conspiracy to exclude noncertified attorneys from reimbursement. The FTC proceedings last over 4 years without resolution. To avoid further legal expenses, MegaCorp and IBB ultimately continue to require specialty certification as a criterion for reimbursement but offer the opportunity to noncertified attorneys to demonstrate equivalent qualifications and thereby receive reimbursement.

MegaCorp, IBB, and the association have incurred substantial legal fees over the 4-year period.

How Does One Minimize Risk to Oneself and to the Association?

The following precautions are recommended:

1. Assure that there is a clear need for any credentialing program instituted by the association, with no suitable alternatives available from other sources, because such a program entails significant legal risks that cannot be completely eliminated.
2. Avoid any "informal" or ad hoc credentialing program not subject to thorough legal review.
3. Assure that criteria for any certification, listing, or other credential are reasonable—that they are based on data or a respected body of professional or educational opinion linking each criterion to the qualities that the credential purports to measure.
4. Establish equivalent criteria or alternative paths to credentialing wherever possible.
5. "Grandfathering" may be acceptable if limited and reasonable.
6. Unlawful discrimination must be avoided; accommodations must be made for the disabled. (See chap. 4, "Discrimination by Federal Grantees.")
7. Care should be taken in promoting programs to avoid disparagement of the noncredentialed. See chapter 7, "Advice and Endorsements," concerning the risks of *endorsing* the services of those who *are* credentialed.
8. Adequate due process must be built into any credentialing program.
9. There must be no bias or partiality in establishing or operating the program.

12

Product Standards, Testing, and Certification

How Do Legal Risks Arise for Associations From Product Quality Endeavors?

Product standardization, testing, and certification are among the oldest and most common activities of United States associations. Since colonial times, groups of businesses have issued statements on common terminology, simplification of parts or styles, and, most typical of all, uniform design or performance specifications. Tens of thousands of association-promulgated product standards are now in place throughout American industry. Associations that have developed product standards have often gone the next step and engaged in testing and certification of products against the established standards. Testing can be performed by the association itself or by commercial or nonprofit laboratories approved or recognized by the association. Although it is most often trade or industry associations that undertake these programs, it is also not unusual for a professional association to develop standards, testing, and certification programs for the products used by the profession. These product quality endeavors have manifest benefits for manufacturers and sellers of products. They raise the level of competition, provide common targets and goals, simplify ordering and communication, help assure interchangeability of parts, and so on. The programs also have very substantial benefits for buyers and users of products. They help upgrade and maintain quality, provide benchmarks for consumers, and often limit the numbers and types of items that must be purchased. Programs of privately issued standards, testing, and certification are always voluntary—there is no compulsion of law for compliance or participation; nevertheless, government agencies have often adopted association product quality programs through mandatory regulations.

Legal problems that can arise from association-sponsored standards, testing, or certification programs are substantial and significant. As one indication of the prominence of the subject, antitrust opinions of the United States Supreme Court have addressed it repeatedly in recent years. Product quality programs can, whether intentionally or inadvertently, restrict competition by limiting the availability of products or services, excluding competitors from a field, affecting pricing and fees, and so on. (See chap. 5, "Antitrust Generally.") There are also potentially serious defamation and product liability risks for associations engaged in these areas of endeavor. (See chaps. 6, "Defamation," 7, "Advice and Endorsements," and 10, "Guidelines, Advisories, Models, or Recommendations.")

Who Is at Risk?

Associations themselves, as well as association volunteers and employees, can be challenged and penalized severely if they have been involved in product quality programs such as standardization, testing, or certification that were used to achieve anticompetitive ends. Penalties paid by associations and association members have reached the seven-figure level in antitrust litigation in the this area, not counting legal defense costs.

What Legal Principles Govern the Area?

The basic legality of association-sponsored standards, testing, and certification programs has frequently been affirmed by courts, which have typically noted the many benefits made available to suppliers, users, and government from the programs. Legal challenges against association product quality programs, however, have also resulted in many instances of liability, from which some general guidelines can be distilled:

1. **Price fixing.** Product standards, testing, and certification programs must not be used as vehicles for raising, lowering, or stabilizing prices.
2. **Boycotts.** The programs must not have a purpose or effect of excluding competitors.
3. **Availability.** They must not be intended for, or result in, limiting production or availability of goods.
4. **Design versus performance.** Design, specification, or construction standards are less preferable than performance standards because the latter permit more latitude and innovation.
5. **Consensus.** Standards should be developed with the input of as wide a group of interested parties as possible and should then be offered for comment to all who will be affected by the standards.
6. **Updating.** Standards should be updated periodically to assure that they reflect state-of-the-art technology.
7. **Voluntariness.** Use of standards, testing, and certification programs must be completely voluntary.
8. **Due process.** Those who oppose or object to association decisions in connection with standards, testing, or certification programs should be afforded notice of the decisions, opportunity to object, and, in some states, appeal of adverse determinations to an impartial body not involved in the original determination.
9. **Conducting testing.** Testing in connection with association standards or certification programs should be by recognized laboratories following objective testing criteria in an unbiased manner; associations sponsoring testing should periodically ensure that the laboratories are fully performing their obligations.
10. **Representations.** There should be no implicit or explicit representations regarding product testing that are not accurate and verifiable;

no attempt should be made to force or require the use of testing or certification by producers or users. (See chaps. 6, "Defamation," and 7, "Advice and Endorsements.")

11. **Membership.** No one should be denied access to a standards, testing, or certification program because of nonmembership in the sponsoring association. (See chap. 13, "Membership.")

12. **Interpretation.** Interpretation of standards, testing, or certification requirements should be nonbiased, unaffected by competitive pressures, and consistent with due process requirements. (See chaps. 1, "Loyalty and Conflicts of Interest," and 7, "Advice and Endorsements.")

Hypothetical Scenarios Concerning Product Quality Programs

The following are examples of fact situations involving association-sponsored standards, testing, and certification programs. They are purely fictional; they are not intended to reflect actual entities or individuals.

Example 1: Undue Influence Over Standards Development

An association of equipment manufacturers proposes to amend a long-standing standard for switching devices; the proposal has been suggested by Onuf, Inc., a firm that manufactures a new form of switching device that it believes is an improvement over old technology but is not encompassed by the association's current standard. When the membership of the association is asked to meet to approve the standards committee's recommendation to amend this standard, representatives of the majority of the association's manufacturer members, which are not yet capable of producing anything similar to Onuf's newer switching devices, "lobby" extensively for a rejection of the proposed amendment, "pack" the meeting with opponents of the amendment, and threaten litigation if the amendment is approved. It is defeated. Onuf, Inc. sues and wins a major antitrust judgment against not only the association but also the members that worked toward defeat of the amendment.

Standards development must be conducted in an environment free of bias and economic pressures. An association engaged in this area of endeavor must establish and adhere to procedures that ensure fair and objective decision making.

Example 2: Testing Laboratories

A national medical specialty association has promulgated performance standards for instrumentation used in its medical specialty. It has also designated several commercial testing laboratories to test instrumentation submitted by manufacturers to determine compliance with the association's standards. Instrumentation which is found to meet the standards may be labeled and promoted as such, a near-requisite for successful marketing to members of the medical specialty. The testing laboratories pay a substantial fee to the association to become designated laboratories and are subject to periodic review and audit by the association to assure the maintenance of quality, accurate, and objective testing services.

The association neglects for several years to check on its designated testing laboratories. Instrumentation reaches the market that is represented as meeting the association's standards but in fact does not. A federal government agency learns of this, brings an administrative action against the association, and compels it to sign a consent order in which the association commits to a protocol of monitoring designated laboratories. Legal and technical consulting fees for the association are substantial.

To avoid this liability, the association should have had clear requirements for designated testing laboratories and should have periodically checked the labs to assure compliance with the requirements.

Example 3: Product Certification

An association in the residential construction industry in the State of Nervonah has for years been on the defensive because of news reports that its members use building products that the manufacturers represent as meeting mandatory government-promulgated standards but in fact do not. The association launches a certification program in which building products that are subject to government standards are tested to see if they actually meet the standards; if found in compliance, the products may then bear the association's logo. The program is open only to manufacturers that become associate-supplier members of the association.

The association concludes that its product certification program would be used even more heavily in the field if it were to become essentially mandatory. It makes presentations to major mortgage lenders in the state, urging that they require use of association-certified building projects as a prerequisite to their mortgage commitments. Eventually, virtually all new residential construction in the State of Nervonah includes association-certified products where government standards apply and the association tests and certifies the products.

A nonmember manufacturer of building products, Ajax, sues the association, arguing that the certification program effectively boycotts Ajax's products by requiring that unnecessary costs be incurred to demonstrate that the products meet government standards when, Ajax alleges, its products already do meet the standards.

The court finds that the association's program is procompetitive and free from legal taint to the extent that it assists in ensuring that only quality building products are used in the State of Nervonah. However, the court finds unreasonable the requirement that manufacturers join the association to take advantage of its certification program. It orders the program to be made available to nonmember manufacturers such as Ajax for a reasonable charge. Each side is ordered to bear its own litigation costs.

How to Limit Risk to the Association and to Individuals

Product standards, testing, and certification programs conducted by associations have often been challenged in court and can expose the associations to significant risk. They must be very carefully structured and managed to minimize legal disputes and maximize the likelihood of success if disputes arise. Some rules should be kept in mind:

1. Keep competitive and economic pressures completely away from product quality programs.
2. Make programs as open as possible.
3. Ensure that broad consensus among the affected community is formed around proposals for standards and criteria, as well as around amendment proposals, with the greatest possible "sunshine" on the process.
4. Reduced volunteer involvement and increased association staff involvement may assist in objectivity and the absence of bias.
5. Ensure that participation in and use of programs are completely voluntary. (See chap. 10, "Guidelines, Advisories, Models, or Recommendations.")
6. Periodically review all standards and criteria to assure that they are current and reflect new technology.
7. Carefully monitor outside consultants, contractors, and laboratories.
8. Ensure that "due process" is provided to those who participate in the programs.
9. Care should be exercised in representations made regarding the products for which an association develops standards or undertakes testing or certification.

13 _____

Membership

How Do Decisions on Membership Eligibility Pose Legal Risks for Associations?

Membership in trade and professional associations is ordinarily available in one or more categories to entities or individuals meeting criteria set out in the associations' bylaws or other governing documents, the associations' membership applications, and the associations' membership solicitation materials. Associations that deny applications for membership or terminate existing members run a high risk of legal challenge unless the reasons for denial or termination are clear, reasonable, and straightforward ones—for example, nonpayment of dues, failure to meet objective definitions of eligibility, or unwillingness to comply with a reasonable code of business or professional ethics. In fact, many associations have in the past been required to defend against legal challenges resulting from adverse membership eligibility decisions. In general, the more important membership in an association is for employment, engagement, sales, work assignment, or reimbursement in a business or profession, the more closely a court will scrutinize membership criteria and procedures and the more readily it will overturn what it perceives to be unreasonable criteria or unfair procedures.

Where association membership is essential, or even very important, for business or professional success, arbitrary exclusion of an applicant can be deemed an illegal boycott, because the decision is considered to be made collectively by a group of entities or individuals, already members of the association, who are in competition with the applicant. (See chap. 5, "Antitrust Generally.")

Who Is at Risk?

Any association volunteer or employee involved in decisions about membership criteria or eligibility, or in deciding whether and the extent to which non-members are entitled to the privileges of membership, could incur personal liability or liability for the association under the theories discussed in this chapter.

What Legal Principles Govern Membership Criteria and Decisions?

There are two main kinds of legal risk to associations from decisions that they make about membership:

1. **Antitrust.** The century-old federal law against "contracts, combinations, and conspiracies in restraint of trade" has often been applied to invalidate denial or termination of association membership. Where a challenger can show that association membership has significant business or professional value and was withheld by the association on arbitrary or unreasonable grounds, the finding of an antitrust violation is likely. A court's conclusion would be that (a) there was a "contract," "combination," or "conspiracy," because an association is by definition a group of competitors; and (b) there was an unreasonable "restraint of trade," in view of the value of the association membership withheld. (See chap. 5, "Antitrust Generally.")

2. **Due process.** Separately or together with the theory of antitrust liability, the denial or termination of association membership can also be overturned on the theory of "fairness"—failure of the association to afford fundamental "due process." While private organizations such as associations are not required to meet the same procedural standards as those applicable to courts, in most states, basic due process requirements apply to association membership decisions and mandate at least (a) *notice* to the person whose membership is to be denied or terminated, and (b) an *opportunity to respond* to the association's notice. Some states may even require, as an element of fundamental due process, that there be *access to an appeals body* not involved in the original adverse decision.

In addition to antitrust and fairness theories, courts have occasionally ordered the reversal of association membership decisions, and the payment of damages by associations for their wrongdoing in making the decisions, on the basis of other theories such as common law equity, defamation (see chap. 6), and discrimination (see chap. 4).

In general, courts are suspicious of membership exclusions of any kind; associations that otherwise expend considerable resources to promote membership necessarily come under close scrutiny when they instead try to exclude those who desire to join. Associations must carefully observe their own criteria and procedures set out in the associations' governing documents in making membership decisions. The following principles reflect those laid down through scores of court decisions involving association membership.

Reasonable Criteria

In establishing or implementing criteria for membership, an association must ensure that the criteria define a valid and recognized business or professional group or subgroup, that the criteria impose limits or boundaries on the definition of the group that are reasonable and not based on personal or competitive motives, and that the criteria are relatively objective and do not easily lend themselves to varying interpretations.

Consistent Application

Eligibility criteria can rarely be totally objective except in the case of larger membership populations (e.g., all those engaged in manufacturing a specific product or all those holding valid licenses in a recognized profession), so some interpretation of criteria is often essential (e.g., when criteria relate to experience or achievement). It is crucial that interpretation and implementation of the criteria be consistent for all those seeking to obtain or retain membership. If waivers of particular requirements are permitted, they must be consistently offered or denied. Inconsistency suggests arbitrariness, which courts will not hesitate to sanction.

No Discrimination

Obviously, membership eligibility decisions based upon discriminatory criteria (e.g., age, gender, race, religion) are extremely suspect and are likely to be overturned upon review. (See chap. 4, "Discrimination by Federal Grantees.")

Safe Harbors

Some kinds of criteria for association membership are appropriate and do not raise legal risks because they are necessary for the operation of the association. They include requirements for submission of applications and other documentation of eligibility, payment of dues or assessments, and adherence to reasonable standards of business or professional ethics (see chap. 8, "Business and Professional Ethics").

Impartiality

Membership eligibility determinations must be made objectively, without the opportunity for personal animosity, anticompetitive motives, or blackballing to become factors in the determinations. Eligibility criteria that include the need for nominations, endorsements, references, referrals, recommendations, or sponsorships must be handled with particular care to avoid improper partiality. The purpose of peer input on a membership eligibility decision should be exclusively to help establish whether the applicant entity or individual meets the published professional criteria, not to establish whether the entity is "on the up and up" or "legitimate" or whether the individual is "well liked" or "socially safe." (See also chap. 1, "Loyalty and Conflicts of Interest.")

Rights of Nonmembers

Although some will find it surprising, associations may even have legal obligations to nonmembers in some, limited circumstances. Where an association offers a service or product that is truly *essential* for one to compete in a field, it can be regarded as an antitrust violation for the association to restrict the service or product to members only. Most of what associations offer their members cannot be said to be essential to competition or may be available elsewhere, even if at higher cost. Some association services or products, however, might well be considered essential and may thus have to be made available upon request to nonmembers who compete with members. It is clear that nonmembers can be charged more for access to the service or product to reflect the fact that members' dues support the association, and there is apparently no requirement that services or products be advertised or promoted to nonmembers.

Hypothetical Membership Scenarios

The following scenarios illustrate the legal risks and principles of association membership eligibility determinations. Any resemblance to actual persons or existing entities is completely unintentional.

Example 1: Impartiality

The membership committee of a state professional association is evaluating an application for membership from Pat Doe, in which Doe provides documentation to attempt to demonstrate that Doe's doctoral degree, from an institution in Albania, is "equivalent" to degrees from U.S. institutions. There is evidence that at least one current member of the association, a former officer, obtained membership on the basis of a doctoral degree from the same institution in Albania, although the records of that membership determination cannot be found. A member of the membership committee, who is seeking an academic appointment in competition with candidate Pat Doe but does not disclose that fact to the membership committee, argues vigorously that Doe is unqualified and "culturally unsuited" to the profession and that the "precedent" of the earlier determination is inadequately documented and should not be followed. The membership committee votes to deny membership to Doe, who subsequently does not receive the academic appointment, either.

Pat Doe sues the association and wins. The court finds both antitrust and discrimination violations. A large judgment is awarded, based on anticipated salary from the academic appointment, which is trebled (multiplied by three) as provided in the antitrust laws. For the committee member who helped sway the decision against Doe, the court finds, there should have been either full disclosure without voting or complete recusal (i.e., nonparticipation) from discussions of the matter. Judgment is rendered against the association because, according to the court, the membership denial was an institutional decision, and procedures should have been in place to eliminate this partiality. In cases of equivalency determinations of requests for waivers, records should be kept of both the decisions and the reasons for the decisions to assist in future similar determinations.

Example 2: Confidentiality

A corporation, American Petroco, submits an application for membership in a national association of raw materials suppliers in the chemical industry; it is required to obtain three written sponsorship letters, which are to be submitted in confidence. One sponsor unexpectedly makes a strong recommendation against membership for American Petroco, citing business impropriety, which later proves to be untrue. Membership is denied. The membership determination and adverse recommendation are later "leaked" and made public.

American Petroco sues for defamation and wins a large award against the association.

The court held that the association was responsible for disclosure of the adverse, untrue information about the applicant and should have taken steps to ensure confidentiality of sponsorship letters.

Example 3: Verification

A representative of a professional association's membership committee, Jones, seeks to verify the accuracy of academic information from Ivy University presented with a candidate's application. In doing so, Jones learns that the Ivy U. transcript submitted is a valid one, but Jones also hears rumors regarding serious academic misconduct by the applicant while enrolled at Ivy U. To avoid the "hassle" of dealing with the problem, Jones simply reports that the candidate's academic record from Ivy is inadequate and unacceptable. Membership is denied.

The candidate challenges the membership decision, and the association is forced to reverse it under the threat of a lawsuit. Although an objective investigation and resolution of the accuracy of the rumors by the association might have led to a denial of membership that could be successfully defended, this "short-cut" could be regarded as arbitrary and legally defective.

Example 4: False Representations

Two members of the association's membership committee, Able and Baker, receive information at the association's annual meeting that the academic credentials of a prominent association member, Dr. Charlie, were deliberately misstated in Charlie's original application for association membership made years earlier. Verification of the inaccuracy of the information originally provided on behalf of Dr. Charlie is obtained by telephone from the academic institution. Charlie is scheduled to present a very prestigious sponsored paper and to receive an award at the association's annual convention. A majority of committee members convene and, inspired by passionate entreaties from Able and Baker, vote to terminate Dr. Charlie's membership. The paper and award presentations are canceled.

Dr. Charlie sues and wins. The court notes that the association's bylaws are very specific regarding these situations. They provide that cases of possible revocation of membership based upon false or fraudulent information at the time of application—or cases of revocation due to unethical conduct prior to membership—*must* be reviewed by the association's ethics committee, with that committee, as distinguished from the membership committee, making a recommendation to the association's governing board, which alone has the authority to revoke membership in such instances. The court finds that, regardless of the substantive merits of the membership committee's summary termination action, it was procedurally faulty.

Example 5: Services to Nonmembers

A trade association has, through a voluntary committee, developed a highly innovative set of worker testing materials that are copyrighted and sold to members only. Over time, all companies that conduct this testing have realized the superiority of the association's materials and have specified that testing in this area be conducted using only those materials. A nonmember human resources consulting firm, Fox Associates, claims that it cannot obtain consulting engagements in this area unless the firm has access to the association's worker testing materials; on this basis, Fox Associates makes a request for the materials. The association agrees to provide the materials to Fox, but only at a very high cost, many times what would be the annual dues for Fox to belong to the association.

Fox Associates brings suit against the association and wins. The testing materials are found to be "essential" to Fox's consulting in the human resources area, and the price at which they were offered to Fox is found to be unrelated to the dues of members that helped support the creation of the materials. A large damages award against the association is entered, and the association is ordered to provide the materials to Fox Associates and other nonmembers at reasonable charges.

How Does One Minimize Risk to Oneself and to the Association?

The following guidelines are recommended:

1. Ensure that association membership eligibility criteria are reasonable and valid.
2. Ensure that the membership criteria are consistently applied to all those seeking to obtain or retain membership and that procedures set out in the association's governing documents are conscientiously followed.
3. Avoid any discrimination or suggestion of discrimination in membership decisions (e.g., discrimination based on age, gender, race, religion).

4. Carefully follow steps to ensure due process protection for those denied membership and for those whose membership is revoked.
5. Ensure that impartiality, bias, or conflicts of interest are not allowed to influence membership eligibility determinations.
6. Make services available to nonmembers in circumstances in which they are essential for doing business or practicing a profession.

Part III

Legal Issues in Professional Practice Programs

Introduction

The chapters in Part III discuss legal issues that arise uniquely in professional associations that assist members in improving and advancing the members' professional practices. All who deal with practice issues in professional associations should be familiar with the issues discussed herein. Chapter 14 addresses fees, reimbursement, and modes of practice; it describes and illustrates the unique risks that arise when professional associations engage in activities that relate to fee, reimbursement, and mode of practice issues. Chapter 15 addresses state licensing. For any professional association whose members are licensed by states, or desire to be licensed by states, this chapter is extremely important. Professional associations have made great strides toward assisting their members through education in practice administration and through governmental and public advocacy; the chapters in Part III will assist volunteers and employees of those associations in making further strides while minimizing legal risks.

14 _____

Fees, Reimbursement, and Modes of Practice

What Are the Legal Concerns for Professional Associations in Addressing Fees, Reimbursement, and Modes of Practice?

Many professional associations once regarded themselves as exclusively scientific, educational, or research organizations. In recent years, however, issues affecting the professional practices of members have increasingly garnered the attention of these associations. Through programs in government affairs, legal affairs, and public affairs, professional associations are now sometimes very aggressive in advancing the practices of their constituencies. They provide education, research, and advocacy regarding many economic, management, marketing, and legal aspects of practice. At times, a professional association's endeavors pertain to fees charged to customers/patients/clients by members, to private and governmental third-party reimbursement for members, and to modes of practice by members. There is much that a professional association can do to assist members in improving their practices in all of these areas, but there are also very serious risks for the association if its endeavors, or those of individuals acting on behalf of the association, stray beyond permissible legal limits.

The century-old antitrust laws in the United States require that decisions that have important effects upon competition must be made by individual competitors rather than by two or more competitors together (see chap. 5, "Antitrust Generally"). The antitrust laws strictly prohibit agreements among competitors on amounts charged, segments served, or relationships avoided, which are termed, respectively, *fee setting*, *allocation*, or *boycotting*, and may be declared illegal per se (i.e., illegal "in and of itself"), regardless of any attempted justification. Enormous penalties are established for antitrust law violations; even the accusation of antitrust wrongdoing by governmental or private challengers subjects the accused to extensive and expensive legal proceedings. Because professional associations already consist of groups of competitors united to engage in joint action, they are, as the Supreme Court has stated, "rife with opportunities" to violate the antitrust laws. These associations must carefully avoid any policies or programs that might raise the specter of antitrust violations in activities regarding fees, reimbursement, or modes of practice.

Who Is at Risk?

Any volunteer or employee of a professional association may incur personal liability or liability for the association by engaging in the kinds of activities discussed in this chapter.

What Legal Principles Govern Activities Regarding Fees, Reimbursement, and Modes of Practice?

1. **Fees.** Price fixing, including fee setting, is the most serious of antitrust violations. It is prosecuted most readily and penalized most severely. The antitrust laws prohibit, as illegal price fixing, any explicit or implicit agreement, such as by members of a professional association, to raise, lower, or stabilize professional fees. The following legal principles govern association activities regarding fees for professional services:

   a. The association, its members, and its employees must avoid any action, program, policy, communication, publication, or other endeavor that even suggests joint decision making by members on professional fees charged to customers/patients/clients.

   b. Caution should be used in conducting and promulgating any research or survey of fees for professional services to ensure that joint fee setting by members is not facilitated and to ensure that there is no exhortation or encouragement of common action by members on specific fees or ranges of fees. Although the federal government has itself promulgated "relative value schedules" in the health care field, measuring the differences in skill and resources necessary to perform various professional services, the federal government has also challenged such endeavors when undertaken by private professional associations.

   c. It is not necessary that competitors reach an open and obvious agreement on fees before they can be held responsible for illegal price fixing; communications regarding joint action on fees followed by parallel conduct on fees consistent with the communications has been found sufficient to violate the law.

   d. An agreement or understanding among competitors on professional fees is illegal even if it is intended to lower or stabilize fees for customers/patients/clients; the Supreme Court has held that an agreement by members of an association of health care professionals to hold down their fee increases at the request of a health care reimburser was illegal price fixing. The "bottom line" is that individual professional competitors must establish their fees individually, not in concert with others.

   e. Agreements among competitors on issues other than fee amounts, where the agreements nevertheless have important effects on fees, are subject to the same antitrust proscriptions; courts and government antitrust enforcers have declared agreements to be illegal when they involved joint fee advertising, common business hours, terms and conditions for payment, refraining from competitive bidding, components of packages of services, and so on.

2. **Third-party reimbursement.** Boycotting is also an extremely serious antitrust violation, one that has frequently been the subject of governmental and private antitrust challenges involving professional as-

sociations. It is illegal for competitors in a profession to agree that they will not deal with other competitor classes, with customer/patient/client populations, or with third-party reimbursers. As third-party payment for health care services becomes increasingly important, for example, associations of health care professionals must search for ways to ensure that reimbursement mechanisms include reasonable coverage provisions, establish reasonable payment levels, and use reasonable claims procedures. They must be vigilant, though, to avoid attempts to "enforce" their views upon third-party reimbursers through actual or threatened boycotts. There is additional leeway in dealings with governmental reimbursement systems such as Medicare and Medicaid, but the extent of that leeway is not clear. The following legal principles govern association activities regarding third-party reimbursement for professional services:

a. It is illegal for members of an association of competitors in a profession to agree to boycott a third-party reimbursement system, such as when the scope of coverage, payment levels, or claims procedures are regarded by the members or by the association as unacceptable.

b. Courts have declared agreements fostered by associations to be illegal when they resulted in members' refusing to follow certain claims procedures or to participate in certain reimbursement systems promulgated by private third-party reimbursers.

c. Even implied threats of boycott may risk investigation or challenge under the antitrust laws, such as when members of an association concur on third-party payment levels and communicate that only such levels are acceptable.

d. There is an exception in the antitrust laws for communications with government in all branches—legislative, judicial, administrative—because those communications are considered to be the exercise of First Amendment rights; it is likely that communications with government branches regarding any aspect of the Medicare and Medicaid third-party reimbursement programs are protected by this right, but the issue is not entirely resolved.

e. Communication of the views of a professional association to nongovernmental reimbursers, such as insurance companies, on the insurers' payments and procedures is tolerated under the antitrust laws, but actual or threatened boycott by the association is not tolerated. An association must be careful that any agreed-upon recommendation on payments by nongovernmental reimbursers does not constitute fee setting.

3. **Modes of practice.** As with fees and third-party reimbursement, there are limits imposed by the antitrust laws on activities of professional associations that affect methods of professional practice by members. An association may certainly engage in some activities that regulate members' practices; an example is the promulgation and enforcement of an ethics code, which clearly protects the public and significantly enhances professional competition among members. (See

chap. 8, "Business and Professional Ethics.") However, many agreements or rules that limit competition without an overriding public interest or procompetitive rationale may well run afoul of the antitrust laws. The following legal principles govern professional association activities regarding modes of practice:

a. As a general principle, members of a professional association must remain free to make decisions affecting their practices, such as where the practices are located, what services are offered in the practices, what colleagues they will practice with, whether they will be employees or owners of the practices, and so on. Association programs that tend to limit this freedom could attract careful legal scrutiny.

b. Association rules or requirements that have the purpose or result of limiting modes of practice—for example, location, practice development endeavors, targeted customer/patient/client populations, group practice arrangements, affiliations with other kinds of professionals—without substantial public interest or procompetitive justification may be illegal and must be avoided.

c. Criticism or discipline by an association of members who engage in modes of professional practice disfavored by the association risks legal challenge on antitrust and other grounds.

Hypothetical Scenarios Concerning Fees, Reimbursement, and Modes of Practice

The following scenarios are purely fictional. They are designed to illustrate the nature of legal risks faced by professional associations, their volunteers, and their employees. Any resemblance to persons living or dead, or to institutions or entities of any kind, is completely unintentional.

Example 1: Fees

A state association of health care professionals has received numerous requests from members, patients of members, consumer protection agencies, the state licensing board, and third-party reimbursers that the association publish a schedule of typical professional fees charged for the health care services most often provided in the practice of this profession. The association commissions a statewide fee survey by a recognized outside surveying firm; the survey results provide average current fees for a list of services in the state. In transmitting the survey results to the association, the outside firm offers its analysis, including the commentary that fees reported for a particular service when provided in a particular area of the state appear to be unreasonably low and likely do not adequately reflect the considerable professional resources required to provide the service. The association promulgates the survey results, with the outside firm's analysis, to members and to nonmember requesters.

An investigation and civil suit is brought against the association by the state antitrust enforcement agency. It alleges that fees for the service provided by members that the association's outside surveying firm had considered to be too low in one area of the state have increased there since the survey results were promulgated. It accuses the association of price fixing and seeks an injunction and fines, as well as treble damages (i.e., three times the actual damages suffered) based on state-funded health care reimbursement programs that cover payment for the service. Following protracted litigation proceedings and a jury trial, the association loses the case and is required to pay substantial fines and damages to the state.

Professional associations that conduct fee surveys should be extremely cautious about all aspects of the endeavors, avoiding particularly any explicit or implicit exhortation to action by association members concerning survey information involving fees.

Example 2: Third-Party Reimbursement

A representative of Ajax Health Insurance, Inc. calls a national medical specialty association and seeks information regarding the association's reaction to a substantial change that Ajax plans to make in its coverage of services provided by association members. In effect, Ajax will cover only the services of specialists who agree to become exclusive providers to Ajax insureds, with their professional fees reimbursed on a fixed annual capitation or per-patient basis. The association executive who takes the call denounces the proposal angrily, suggests a "war" by association members against Ajax, and "guarantees" that no member will be willing to comply with Ajax's proposed reimbursement conditions. The executive notes further that the association will include a critical article about the Ajax proposal in an upcoming association publication. The discussion ends in a heated argument.

Ajax reports the incident to the Federal Trade Commission (FTC), which launches a 2-year investigation into all of the medical specialty association's policies and programs regarding third-party reimbursement. The FTC makes clear throughout the investigation that the association is free to comment on reimbursement matters as long as the comments do not constitute fee setting but that the association must not threaten or conduct a boycott of third-party reimbursers. Ultimately, the association signs a consent order in which it does not admit to wrongdoing but agrees to make no explicit or implicit threats to health care reimbursers. The FTC press releases regarding the consent order are carried by the general press nationwide; the association's costs and legal fees are significant, as is the expenditure of staff time on the matter.

Example 3: Boycotts

At the national convention of an association of licensed residential property appraisers, several members of the governing board discuss a recent announcement by a major national mortgage lending company in which fixed, "flat" fees are established by the company for appraisal services that the company purchases around the country. The association board members unani-

mously agree that the fee levels are deplorable. The board members' views
find their way into a convention newsletter published by the association and
are characterized there as representing the views of the association. There is
a marked fall-off in the availability of appraisers who are willing to work with
this mortgage lending company. The company complains to the Department
of Justice Antitrust Division, accusing the association of engaging in an illegal
boycott.

The Justice Department begins a criminal investigation of the matter. It
calls all the members of the governing board of the association, as well as its
senior employed executives, as witnesses before a federal grand jury; each is
separately represented by his or her own legal counsel reimbursed by the
association, although legal counsel are not permitted to accompany the witnesses into the grand jury sessions. The Justice Department refuses to identify
the targets of its investigation, so that each witness lives for over a year with
the anxiety of a possible criminal indictment. Ultimately, the Justice Department ends the investigation with no explanation.

How Does One Minimize Risk to Oneself and to the Association?

1. Use extreme caution in any endeavors of a professional association
   that involve professional fees; when in doubt, avoid the subject and
   seek legal assistance through the association.
2. Avoid not only association policies or programs intended to achieve
   agreement on raising fees but also those intended to achieve agreement on lowering or stabilizing fees.
3. Plan carefully any research or surveys regarding members' fees to
   minimize the risk of fee-setting challenges; publication of results should
   never include explicit or implicit exhortations to action regarding specific fees or ranges of fees.
4. Avoid activities or endeavors designed to reach consensus or understanding on issues closely related to fees, such as the terms of payment
   required of customers/patients/clients.
5. Do not get together within the association or elsewhere to engage in
   anticompetitive boycotts, exclusions, or refusals to deal with others,
   such as third-party reimbursers; even threatened or implied boycotts
   can become the subjects of legal challenges.
6. Refrain from criticizing features of nongovernmental reimbursement
   plans in ways that members might interpret as a call to boycott.
7. Do not organize members to refuse collectively to follow reimbursers'
   claims requirements or to refuse collectively to participate in reimbursement plans (although individual member action in these areas
   is ordinarily without legal risk).
8. Avoid attempts to dictate members' modes or methods of practice without significant public interest or procompetitive benefit; when in doubt,
   check with legal counsel through the association.

15 ——————————————————————

State Licensing

What Are the Legal Concerns for Associations in Dealing With State Licensing of Professionals?

Licensing of professionals to engage in their professions, or to use professional designations, is a function of state governments, as distinct from private, non-governmental organizations such as associations. State licensing is conducted through boards, agencies, or commissions that are established by state law, that are required to follow state government procedures, and, of particular significance, that enjoy state governmental immunity from many kinds of legal liability. Private associations, by comparison, are exposed to legal liability risks in many areas, such as antitrust and defamation. Association volunteers and employees must remain aware, when dealing in the area of state licensing, that their association's own activities are not protected by governmental immunity, even when similar activities of the state licensing board are protected. It is important to remember, however, that an association is afforded far greater legal latitude when urging the government to adopt a particular licensing standard or other restriction on professional practice or professional designations than when merely promulgating or enforcing rules on its own.

An association's relationship with the state licensing process is often an indirect one. Association programs such as accreditation of education and enforcement of ethics codes are sometimes adopted or referred to by state licensing boards in their regulation of professions. The relationship can be more direct, however, such as when associations attempt to influence the criteria and procedures used by state licensing boards. This chapter summarizes the risks and concerns for associations in the area of state licensing.

Who Is at Risk?

Association volunteers and employees should be familiar with the principles discussed in this chapter if they play any roles with respect to state licensure.

What Legal Principles Apply to Associations' Dealings With State Licensing?

There are several legal principles that govern the relationship of a private professional association with a state governmental licensing board:

1. **First Amendment protection.** An association and its representatives have a First Amendment right to address, petition, advocate, lobby, and otherwise attempt to influence the standards and processes used in state licensing of professionals. The antitrust laws generally do not restrict efforts by associations to petition government for legislation or for administrative or judicial action, even if the actions they seek could be deemed "anticompetitive." A private association's legal leeway is *greatest* when seeking in good faith to influence government.

2. **"Sham" approaches to government.** The Supreme Court has held that excessive, unfounded, or "sham" attempts to intervene in state regulatory proceedings for anticompetitive aims, however, are not protected by the First Amendment from antitrust challenge. Generally, a "sham" attempt is an effort that *appears* to be directed at influencing government decision making but is *in fact* intended to impose a restraint on competitors through purely private means.

3. **Association "self-regulation."** "Self-regulation" endeavors of private entities such as professional associations must be distinguished from regulatory endeavors of governmental entities, such as state licensing boards; even essentially identical programs of credentialing, peer review, fee mediation, and so forth are immunized from most kinds of legal challenges when conducted by a licensing board but not when conducted by an association.

4. **State adoption of association endeavors.** Policies or programs of professional associations that are susceptible to legal challenges are not immunized from those challenges on the basis that the policies or programs are adopted by state governmental licensing boards; an association's ethics enforcement, educational accreditation, and other such programs must be beyond legal reproach, because use of them in governmental licensing generally does not protect an association from challenges to the association's role in developing or conducting the programs.

Hypothetical Licensing Scenarios

The following scenarios illustrate the legal risks and principles of dealing with state licensing. Any resemblance to actual persons or existing entities is completely unintentional.

Example 1: Advocacy

A national association of widget engineers learns that a state licensing board in engineering is considering extending the availability of licensing to those who have not completed an association-accredited specialty educational program in widget engineering; licensing and use of the denomination "Widget Engineer" would be available in the state to anyone who completes 2 years of education or its equivalent in any engineering field from any nonprofit or commercial educational institution in the state. The association launches a major campaign to convince the state board as well as the legislature and governor of the state that this dilution of licensing standards for widget engineers would have serious adverse consequences for citizens. The campaign is successful; the board abandons the proposal. A bill is passed by the legislature and signed into law by the governor, prohibiting consideration of such proposals in the future. Some of the statistics and statements used by the association in the campaign were supplied by outside consultants and later prove to have been exaggerated or unfounded. The unsuccessful proponents of the changes sue the association on antitrust grounds, arguing that the association boycotted for competitive and financial goals all candidates for licensure by the state who were not trained in programs accredited by the association.

The association defends and wins the suit. The court declares that the association has a First Amendment right to advocate its positions to government bodies, even when the positions are based upon exaggerated information.

Example 2: Immunity

A proposal is presented to the House of Delegates of a national association of health care professionals that would amend the association's model legislation for state licensing of its member professionals to prohibit practice in certain managed-care settings. In the past, the association's model legislation has not been binding upon any state but has been widely followed on other issues by most state licensing boards around the country. The proposal in the House of Delegates is highly controversial. Its proponents are able to have it considered by the House during a break in the regular proceedings when many delegates who oppose the proposal are absent from the body's meeting room. They shout down all opposition to the proposal, and they achieve several questionable parliamentary rulings that ensure passage of the proposal, although a later survey suggests that only a small minority of the entire House of Delegates actually favored the proposal.

Some members of the association fear that state licensing law changes consistent with the association's model legislation could bar them from employment and engagements. They are advised by their counsel that there is little hope of success in suing state boards to prevent them from adopting the changes, so instead, they sue the association to have the model legislation declared in violation of the antitrust laws. The association defends on the basis that the model legislation is intended to be used by state government entities, which are immune from antitrust challenge. The association argues that it should be immune as well. The association loses the suit, and the model legislation provisions are declared illegal. The association is ordered to amend the legislation and to pay the plaintiffs' litigation expenses.

There is no protection from liability for associations, their volunteers, or their employees by virtue of the fact that the associations' actions regarding licensing may be adopted by a state government.

Example 3: Government Action Versus Association Action

Version A. Several state licensing boards in a profession decide to initiate fee mediation programs. In these programs, fee mediation services are offered without charge to clients of professionals regulated by the boards when the clients complain about fees and request mediation services. The national association for the profession, recognizing the desirability of having such programs available to clients of members in all states, institutes them in the states where licensing boards have not yet done so. The association's fee mediation programs are identical in all respects to the programs offered by state licensing boards. A private suit is brought by a consumer group against the association and all of the state licensing boards that operate the fee mediation programs, arguing that the programs are biased because of insufficient consumer representation. The suit alleges numerous violations of the antitrust laws arising from the programs.

The licensing boards move to be dismissed from the suit on the basis of their governmental immunity. The court dismisses the boards, and the suit proceeds against the association alone, because the association is not entitled to dismissal on the basis of governmental immunity.

Version B. Instead of instituting private fee mediation services in the remaining states as in Version A, the national association launches an aggressive lobbying campaign intended to persuade the licensing boards in those states to adopt a fee mediation service. In response to the campaign, numerous boards do so, and the consumer group sues. The association's motion to dismiss the suit is granted; the association is found to have merely petitioned government in good faith pursuant to its First Amendment right, and as such cannot be liable solely because those efforts were successful.

How Does One Minimize Risk to Oneself and to the Association?

The following are recommended:

1. Association activities with respect to professional standards and other aspects of state licensing boards should generally be restricted to petitioning efforts directed unambiguously toward modification, clarification, or enforcement of the law (including statutes, regulations, and any other form of law) by legitimate governmental authorities.
2. These activities should be undertaken for the purpose of modifying or enforcing the law and not for any ulterior anticompetitive purpose. (See chap. 5, "Antitrust Generally.")
3. Association-proposed licensure criteria should be reasonable, that is, based upon objective grounds, such as empirical data or a respected body of professional or educational opinion.
4. Legal review of licensure proposals is essential.

Part IV

Legal Issues in Business Price and Cost Programs

Introduction

The chapters in Part IV discuss legal concerns that arise especially for trade associations when they assist members in improving their businesses. Chapter 16 addresses surveys of prices and costs, as well as statistical surveys of all kinds undertaken by associations, with a focus on how to conduct surveys in ways that reduce legal risks, particularly antitrust risks. Chapter 17 deals with discussions at trade association meetings. All associations conduct meetings; it is inevitable that business people discuss business matters at those meetings. This chapter assists associations in ensuring that those discussions will not result in untoward legal consequences for the associations that organize and sponsor the meetings. All who have responsibilities for trade associations, whether volunteers or employees, should become familiar with the guidelines provided in Part IV.

16

Surveys of Prices or Costs

What Are the Risks From Association Surveys of Prices and Costs?

Many trade associations have as one of their central activities the collection and dissemination of information about prices, costs, credit risks, production or sales levels, or other statistics about the businesses or industries represented by the associations. Indeed, statistical surveying was one of the main reasons that trade associations were originally formed during the early history of the United States. Businesses and industries benefit from learning about average or composite data against which to measure their own progress and success or lack of success. Surveys of data and information about the field represented by an association can be undertaken with little legal risk if some important guidelines are carefully observed. These programs can raise liability risks for associations. The U.S. Supreme Court determined in 1925 in the seminal case, *Maple Flooring Manufacturers Association v. the United States,* that the exchange of information among business people actually spurs competition; the antitrust laws are only violated, the Court said, when the information exchanged becomes the basis for anticompetitive agreements among the recipients of the information. In short, trade associations should be encouraged to assist member companies by conducting surveys of important information, but they must also be warned about the serious pitfalls from improperly using that information.

Who Is at Risk?

Associations themselves can incur antitrust liability from the collection and dissemination of business information for anticompetitive purposes (see chap. 5, "Antitrust Generally"). There are also other potential risks from surveying activities, such as defamation risks, for example, when credit information is exchanged that is damaging and inaccurate (see chap. 6, "Defamation"). Association volunteers and employees could also conceivably incur personal liability if they were to participate in activities raising antitrust or other legal concerns.

What Legal Principles Govern the Surveying of Business Information by Associations?

Several principles or guidelines emerge from the numerous court cases, primarily older cases, in which associations were challenged legally in connection with the collection and dissemination to members of business information such as the prices or costs of products or services.

1. **Illegal use of statistics.** Most important of all is the antitrust concern. Information surveys by associations must not be used to effect or facilitate illegal agreements among members to fix prices or terms of sale; establish uniform production levels; allocate markets or customers; or boycott suppliers, competitors, or customers. There is also the risk that dissemination of inaccurate data could involve defamation.

2. **Precautions against misuse.** Associations can become drawn into antitrust investigations or lawsuits when members use association-sponsored price or cost surveys as the bases for the members' own anticompetitive arrangements; thus, the following steps should be taken to minimize the ability of members to use association-published statistical information for illegal ends:

   a. Only gross sales, or average prices or costs, or other composites should be reported in an association's dissemination of statistical information.

   b. No composite data should be reported in a category where only a few submissions were received, thereby permitting the submitters to gauge their competitors' submissions as well.

   c. Individual submissions should be accorded confidentiality; ideally, the individual submissions should be discarded once they have been used to determine the reportable composite data.

   d. Only past information, not projected future prices or costs, for example, should be reported so that this information is not used to influence future prices actually charged.

   e. Participation in any statistical program should be voluntary; there must be no direct or indirect coercion to participate. Distribution of results can be limited to those who provide input to the program.

   f. There must be no explicit or implicit agreement by members or other users to take action in response to the data published by the association.

   g. Association staff should not have discretion to make subjective determinations of composites, missing data, and so on.

   h. In publishing statistical information, neither the association nor any volunteers, employees, or consultants should make exhortations or recommendations for action by members based on the information.

3. **Credit reporting.** Association programs in which credit risk information is exchanged among the members are susceptible to serious abuses and raise special risks of defamation claims. The following precautions are warranted:

   a. Great care must be taken to ensure that the information reported is accurate; submitters might be asked to warrant the accuracy of the information on past due accounts and possibly even to indemnify the association for liability resulting from inaccurate reporting; it is best to report only objective information (such as balances and dates of past due accounts), not subjective comments of creditors.

b. There must be no suggestion or recommendation to recipients of the credit risk information that they refrain from doing business with those whose credit is reported as deficient.

c. Where customers or buyers have their accounts reported by an association as deficient but those customers or buyers are also disputing the deficiencies, consideration should be given by the association to surveying and reporting that factor as well.

d. A measure of protection is afforded by having the credit information collected and disseminated by an outside firm, as distinguished from association staff.

e. If consumer credit, rather than business credit, is reported in an association program, federal or state laws on consumer credit reporting may apply.

4. **Availability.** Results of association statistical programs, if they become very important or essential for doing business in a field and if they cannot be replicated elsewhere, will have to be made available to nonmembers as well as to members. Nonmembers can be charged more than members for participation to reflect members' dues support for the program.

Hypothetical Scenarios on Association Price and Cost Surveys

The following scenarios are hypothetical and fictional; they are provided for illustration purposes only. They are not intended to reflect any actual persons, entities, or situations.

Example 1: Misuse of Statistics

The national association of widget manufacturers has for decades issued monthly reports, compiled by the association's accountants based on submissions by manufacturer members, on members' prices, production levels, sales, and costs. Unbeknownst to the association and its employees, several of the larger members of the association have developed a scheme whereby the association's statistics are used as "signals" to control increases or decreases in widget prices and production levels—that is, a complex mathematical formula has long been in place that gives direction to each widget manufacturer participating in the conspiracy as to when and how it must raise or lower prices and production levels, with greater-than-formula fluctuations permitted on a monthly basis as long as the quarterly average statistics of each firm are consistent with the formula. The widget manufacturer participants credit the arrangement with saving the industry from ruinous price wars, costly fluctuations in production, and unwarranted changes in anticipation of or in response to other companies' business decisions.

Bill Armistead, recently retired vice president of sales for Amalgamated

Widgets, Inc., one of the top three firms in the industry, has a dispute with his firm over retirement benefits; when no satisfactory resolution is forthcoming from Amalgamated, Armistead approaches the Antitrust Division of the U.S. Department of Justice and describes what he knows about the long-standing antitrust conspiracy among widget manufacturers in return for personal immunity from prosecution. A grand jury investigates and indicts the companies that have participated in the conspiracy and several senior executives from each, although not the association. All of the companies and individuals eventually plead guilty, and they receive sentences of fines and jail terms, respectively. Among the penalties imposed on the companies is one prohibiting them from participation in statistical programs for the widget industry. The association's program is terminated permanently.

There is little an association can do to prevent secret antitrust conspiracies on the part of determined members, but the association's leadership should be alert to the possibility, statistical programs should be designed to minimize the possibility, and members should be periodically warned about the antitrust risks.

Example 2: Credit Reporting

An association of computer software providers conducts a program to assist members in managing their accounts receivable; all members are encouraged, but not required, to fill out quarterly reports for the association in which they identify customer accounts over ninety days past due; the association compiles the reports and lists all accounts reported by three or more submitters; only members who provided reports to the association receive the association's monthly compilation; the program is not offered to nonmembers because competing credit reports are available in the industry from commercial sources.

One member of the association, Alpha, is particularly angry with a former customer, Beta, because Beta has threatened to change from Alpha to a competitor to obtain computer software; Alpha provides a fictitious and damaging monthly credit report on the association's form regarding Beta, and it has two affiliates, each of whom happens to maintain separate association membership, do the same. As a result of the association's publication of information on its apparently deficient creditworthiness, Beta is unable to purchase computer software from other association members except under very burdensome terms. Beta learns of the association's compilation, issues a complaint against the association and threatens to approach government authorities. The association, with the assistance of Alpha, makes a substantial settlement payment to Beta. It modifies its credit reporting program rules to ensure that reports from subsidiaries and affiliates of a member company are treated as coming from the company itself.

Example 3: Document Retention

An association in the telecommunications industry uses an outside surveying firm to compile composite statistical information regarding changes in industry sales volume levels on a quarterly basis. The association's staff receives members' reports directly and in confidence so that staff can remind delinquent members to submit their reports, can follow up with incomplete or unclear reports, and so on. Copies of members' reports are provided by staff to the outside firm that prepares the compilations; the originals are kept on file permanently by the association for possible future reference.

Two major companies in the industry, both members of the association and participants in its statistical program, announce their plans to merge; the Federal Trade Commission (FTC) challenges the merger as anticompetitive. The FTC issues a subpoena to the association seeking all of its background documents on the two companies for the previous 10 years, including particularly the quarterly reports on sales volume that the companies submitted over the years and that were used for the industry statistical compilations. The association opposes the subpoena but is unsuccessful. It must expend substantial resources in submitting the documents to the FTC: Even more important, other members learn of the involuntary disclosure to the FTC by the association, and many cease permanently their participation in the compilation program, which as a result must be canceled.

The association, of course, should not have maintained the individual survey submissions on file once they had been used to develop the statistical compilations.

How Does One Limit Risks to the Association and Its Representatives?

Association surveys of prices, costs, and other statistical information, such as creditworthiness, can be of substantial benefit to members, but a few rules must be kept in mind to avoid legal entanglements:

1. Protect against use of association statistics by recipients to effect anticompetitive arrangements.
2. Keep individual members' information confidential.
3. Avoid publication of inaccurate and damaging information or statistics regarding individuals, entities, products, or services.
4. Avoid making recommendations, suggestions, or exhortations to action or response by the recipients as a result of the statistics reported by the association.
5. Limit survey subjects to historical, rather than projected, information.
6. Consider using an outside agent to collect and compile statistical information for association programs.
7. Particularly for credit reporting programs, consider requiring submitters to warrant the accuracy of credit information they submit, reporting billing disputes, and limiting reports to information corroborated by several sources.

17 _____

Discussions at Meetings

What Are the Legal Risks From Discussions at Association Meetings?

Trade associations of every kind and size hold meetings. Meetings may be the most universally common activity of associations at the national, state, and local levels. There are conventions, seminars, trade shows/exhibitions/expositions, symposiums, board and committee meetings, and other gatherings of members. Meetings are one of the most important ways for associations to fulfill their essential mission of assisting members in communicating to one another, networking with one another, and learning from one another. Beyond communication, networking, and education, of course, additional association meetings are necessary to plan and carry out the governance functions of associations.

Extensive discussions occur at trade association meetings among firms that are engaged in business competition; therefore, association meetings present unique opportunities for violations of the law to occur. Antitrust conspiracies can be, and often have been, developed through discussions at trade association meetings (see chap. 5, "Antitrust Generally"). Defamation can occur, product liability can be incurred, and other legal risks are present (see chaps. 6, "Defamation," 7, "Advice and Endorsements," and 10, "Guidelines, Advisories, Models, or Recommendations").

Associations must be acutely aware of the potential risks of facilitating unlawful behavior due to the frequent assembly at association meetings of business competitors for what the associations nevertheless intend and expect to be lawful behavior. Precautions are warranted to avoid or minimize association liability.

Who Is at Risk?

Associations themselves, as well as volunteers and employees of associations, are at potential risk of legal liability from discussions of association members at meetings.

What Legal Principles Apply?

Awareness and understanding of several legal principles can assist association volunteers and employees in minimizing the risk that liability will arise from discussions among participants at association meetings.

1. **Management of discussions at meetings.** It is obvious that associations are not always in control of what discussions might occur among members at meetings sponsored by the associations. Questions and answers exchanged between the podium and the audience at educational sessions, conversations at social events surrounding educational or governance meetings, and off-agenda items raised by participants at board or committee meetings are difficult or impossible to "police." Associations do risk being held responsible for whatever discussions they *can* control, however,—program content of educational sessions, agendas of governance meetings, and so on. Association volunteers and employees should be careful to ensure that, at least when they are in charge of what is discussed at association meetings, there is due regard paid to the legal ramifications of those discussions.

2. **Agreements.** In the antitrust context, courts have often stretched to find that attendees at meetings have "agreed" upon joint anticompetitive business conduct. It is certainly not necessary, when government or private challengers are attempting to prove an antitrust conspiracy, to show that the alleged conspirators actually signed a document committing themselves to illegal conduct, or even to show that they agreed clearly in conversations to commit to the conduct. Discussions at meetings in which the plans for a conspiracy were "signaled" among the meeting attendees, followed by parallel anticompetitive activity of the attendees consistent with the discussions, has been sufficient to support a finding of an antitrust "contract, combination, or conspiracy" in violation of the law. It is thus essential for associations to avoid, to the extent possible, discussions in which business competitors attending association meetings are "signaling" their illegal intentions.

3. **Apparent authority.** It has also been made clear by the U.S. Supreme Court that volunteers and employees of an association can commit the association to organizational antitrust liability if they only "appear" to be acting or speaking on behalf of the association and the association's leadership neither knew of the activities or conversations, approved of them, or benefited from them (see chap. 3, "Apparent Authority"). It is thus crucial for associations to be highly selective in vesting their volunteers and employees with authority to act or speak on behalf of the associations.

Hypothetical Scenarios on Discussions at Meetings

The following scenarios illustrating the legal risks from discussions at association meetings are purely hypothetical; they are not intended to reflect actual persons or entities.

Example 1: Minutes

At the regular quarterly meeting of the Board of Directors of a state association of retailers, Sandy Steamer is recognized by the Chair for a matter under "new business." Steamer heatedly remarks that chain discounters are eroding the customer bases of all independent retailers in the state and suggests that the association organize the independents to jointly put pressure on key suppliers by demanding that they stop selling to the chains or risk losing the business of the independents. The Chair promptly ends the discussion and warns Steamer of its impropriety. There is no further discussion of the matter at this or any other meeting of the state association.

Staff of the association, which routinely makes tape recordings of Board of Directors meetings to assist staff in writing the minutes, has recorded this exchange at the Board meeting.

Several independent retailers in the state, including Steamer, later organize an effort, completely outside of the association, to boycott suppliers who sell to the discounting chains. Antitrust litigation is brought by the chains against these independents. The association is made a codefendant in the suit. Not only its minutes, but also the tape recording of the Board of Directors meeting at which Steamer urged an association-sponsored boycott, must be provided to the plaintiffs in discovery.

The association is ultimately dismissed from the litigation, but not before it has expended substantial legal defense costs. Its dismissal is delayed for months because of arguments among the litigants over the possible role of the association in the conspiracy as evidenced by the tape recording. The other defendants make major settlement payments to resolve the litigation.

Association volunteers and employees must remain vigilant about discussions at meetings that might raise legal concerns. Here, the leadership acted appropriately, of course, but its practice of routine maintenance of meeting recordings beyond the time when the recordings were needed to write minutes may have doomed the association to greater involvement in the litigation than otherwise might have been the case.

Example 2: Agreement

A national association representing businesses that serve as commissioned sales agents has an extensive statistical reporting program. Each of the association's members appoints a representative, ordinarily the member's head of sales and marketing, to sit on the association's statistical committee. The committee meets regularly to go over the statistical reports before they are disseminated by the association.

At one meeting of the statistical committee, a committee member, Washington, notes that the statistics clearly demonstrate that members' commission revenues are decreasing while members' costs are increasing. Washington says that, whatever the other members of the association decide to do, his firm plans to raise its commission levels by 10% within the following 2 weeks. Other members of the committee note their agreement with Washington's assessment of the statistics, but none of the others vow, as Washington did, to raise commission rates. In fact, however, within the following 2 weeks, virtually all of the businesses represented on the committee take action to raise their commission levels, usually by about 10%.

When some of these firms' customers complain, the Antitrust Division of the U.S. Department of Justice brings a criminal antitrust price-fixing case against all of the companies that had raised their commissions, as well as the association; the individuals who had attended the association's statistical committee meeting are made defendants also. Ultimately, the businesses pay six-figure fines, and the individuals serve 6-month jail terms. The association is bankrupted by the costs of the defense and is ultimately dissolved.

Extreme care must be exercised by those in charge of association meetings to ensure that discussions do not effect or facilitate antitrust conspiracies or other illegal conduct.

How Can One Minimize Legal Risk to Oneself and the Association?

1. **Planned and organized discussions.** Both educational and governance meetings of associations should be conducted according to uniform procedures. There should be notice provided in advance to attendees regarding the subject matter of the meetings; there should be agendas or programs prepared, distributed, and maintained; and there should be minutes taken of governance meetings. Although it is impossible to "script" association meetings, participants should be encouraged to focus on the announced meeting agenda or program.

2. **Awareness and education.** Volunteers who represent business members of associations ordinarily rotate through positions on boards or committees; they are often unaware of the special risks that arise from meetings among competitors at association meetings. Without unduly repressing or inhibiting discussions, association employees responsible for managing meetings should take steps to make sure that attendees are aware of legal risks. Periodic educational endeavors, such as sessions on legal compliance when new board or committee members are oriented, distribution of legal compliance reminders at board or committee meetings, and presentations by association legal counsel at board or committee meetings should be considered.

3. **Participation by staff and/or counsel.** Ordinarily, any meeting sponsored by an association in which education is offered or governance activities occur should be attended by an appropriate staff member of the association. Certain educational or governance meetings on subjects that may raise sensitive legal issues should also be attended by association legal counsel. Many trade and business associations have legal counsel attend all meetings of the associations' governance board for purposes of both monitoring the proceedings to ensure legal compliance and providing input on agenda items discussed at the meetings that might have legal ramifications.

4. **Careful management of meeting records.** Minutes of association meetings can be extremely important in investigations or proceedings in which associations are accused of illegal conduct. Minutes represent

the permanent, formal record of what actually happened—what actually was discussed and resolved—at an association meeting. Minutes should be carefully edited to limit the content to summaries of communications, reports, and resolutions; notes used to prepare drafts of minutes, as well as nonfinal drafts themselves, should not be maintained; there should ordinarily be no transcripts, recordings, or other verbatim versions maintained of the association governance meeting proceedings except the final version; and those who participate at a meeting should be given the opportunity to review and approve the minutes at a subsequent meeting.

Part V

Legal Issues in Publishing

Introduction

Chapter 18 in Part V is on the legal liabilities that can arise for associations that engage in publishing activities, as most associations do. In contrast with the previous four chapters, two of which focus on singular legal risks faced by professional associations and two of which focus on those faced by trade associations, this chapter is important to all associations, professional or trade, that engage in publishing. Chapter 18 covers copyrights issues in particular, both from the point of view of ensuring copyright protection for association materials and of ensuring that the copyrights of others are not violated in the course of association publishing. Chapter 18 should be reviewed carefully by volunteers and employees of associations who have responsibilities in the area of publishing.

18

Publications and Copyright Law

How Does Copyright Law Affect Associations?

Every trade or professional association, through its volunteer and staff leaders, regularly creates and distributes a wide variety of published or recorded materials, ranging from journals, magazines, newsletters, manuals, books, and bulletins to audio- or videotaped presentations of association meetings programs or other subjects. Production of these materials helps an association to carry out its tax-exempt functions; it may contribute substantially as well to the revenues of the association.

Copyright law plays a central role in an association's creation and use of published or recorded materials. Copyright law allows the association to assert exclusive rights in "original works of authorship," which, in turn, permit the association to charge fees for the purchase or use of the material and to prohibit the creation of unauthorized copies. In contrast, however, copyright law also prevents an association from reproducing or otherwise using the original works of others without prior permission except under special circumstances. One who makes unauthorized use of copyrighted material is a copyright "infringer." Remedies available to copyright owners from copyright infringers include "actual damages"—an amount of money calculated as compensation for the injury caused by the infringement—plus infringers' profits, or "statutory damages," as high as $100,000 per "willful" infringement, recovery of costs and attorney's fees, injunctive relief, and the destruction of infringing materials. The federal Copyright Act also provides for criminal penalties against persons or entities that knowingly violate the copyright laws.

Who Is at Risk?

An association is at risk of violating a copyright anytime it makes unauthorized use of copyrighted material owned by another party. All publications and recorded works of an association are fully subject to the copyright laws.

What Legal Principles Govern the Field of Copyright?

1. **A bundle of rights.** A copyright holder owns a variety of rights with respect to the copyrighted material, including the rights to reproduce, distribute, publicly perform, and publicly display the work, as well as the right to prepare "derivative works" based upon the copyrighted

work. For example, each of several functions related to a speech—
to photocopy the speech, to deliver it at an association meeting, to
adapt it into an article for publication in the association's magazine
or journal, or to include it in an edited book compiling similar speeches—
is subject to an *exclusive, separate* right enjoyed by the person or
entity that owns the copyright in the speech.

2. **Tangible medium.** In order to be eligible for copyright protection, a
work must be both original and fixed in a "tangible medium of expression" (e.g., on paper, tape, computer software). Copyrightable works
range from scientific articles to literature to music to motion pictures.

3. **Originality.** Copyright protection is available only for "original works
of authorship." A high degree of originality is not necessary to render
a work eligible for copyright protection, but certain works lack the
necessary originality to render them protectable. For example, a white
pages telephone directory arranged in a simple, alphabetical order
has insufficient originality to qualify for copyright protection. The
key to protectability is the *originality of "expression,"* not the hard
work that may have been expended by the work's creator in order to
discover the facts conveyed in the expression. Nor are the underlying
facts, ideas, procedures, or the like themselves protectable under
copyright law (although they may in some circumstances be protected
under the law of patents, trade secrets, or "unfair competition").

4. **Duration.** Copyright protection begins at the moment in which an
"original work" is "fixed" in a "tangible medium of expression." It is
not necessary to add a copyright notice to the work or register the
work with the federal government in order to own a copyright in the
work—although there are distinct advantages to these procedures,
as discussed later. Thus, a copyright interest is created automatically
upon the act of writing an article or a book or recording a speech.

   For works created after January 1, 1978, the duration of copyright
protection turns on the nature of the work. If the work is a "work
made for hire," as described later, the period of copyright protection
is 75 years from the year of publication or 100 years from the year
of creation, whichever expires first. If the work was created by an
individual author and does not qualify as a "work made for hire,"
then copyright protection lasts for the life of the author plus 50 years.

5. **Ownership of a "work made for hire."** Under the "work made
for hire" doctrine, an association or other employer is deemed to be
the original copyright owner of a work prepared by an employee
within the scope of his or her employment. The association may also
be deemed to be the original copyright owner under the work made
for hire doctrine if (a) the work was specially ordered or commissioned
as a contribution to a collective work, such as a magazine, journal,
or book and (b) the association and the author expressly agree, in a
written document signed by both of them, that the work will be
considered a work made for hire. Under the work made for hire
doctrine, with written agreement between the association and the

author, the association can also become the copyright owner of eight other categories of works specified in the Copyright Act. Among these categories are instructional texts, tests, and testing materials.

The work made for hire doctrine poses special challenges for an association, which ordinarily conducts its educational and communication endeavors using the efforts of a diverse group of individuals. An association's volunteer leaders, consultants, third-party service providers, and others who from time to time are retained to create articles, booklets, tapes, or other copyrightable materials, are generally not employees. When a nonemployee is retained by an association to create a work, the work made for hire doctrine will recognize the association as the owner of the copyright *only* if the work is among the nine categories set forth in the Copyright Act *and* the parties agree in writing that the work will be treated as a work for hire.

6. **Ownership through written assignment of copyright.** Even when a work does not qualify as a work made for hire, the association may obtain copyright ownership through a written assignment signed by the original copyright owner. Mere transfer of a material object in which the copyrighted work is embodied (e.g., a copy of an article or a tape) does *not* result in the recipient's ownership of the copyright. Assignment of copyright occurs *only* if there is a written document signed by the copyright owner reflecting the copyright assignment.

7. **Copyright licenses.** An association can enjoy some of the benefits of copyright without copyright ownership; it can obtain from the copyright owner a license, transferring something less than the entire copyright interest to the association. For example, an association and a third-party author may enter into a formal licensing arrangement that permits the association to exercise (on either an exclusive or nonexclusive basis) any or all of the copyright privileges. A formal, written licensing arrangement is not required; an oral license is legally binding. The disadvantage of an oral license, of course, is that the parties may later have differing recollections of the existence or terms of the license.

In fact, even in the absence of a written or oral license, an association may in certain circumstances enjoy an "implied license" to use a work. With respect to "contributions to collective works," such as articles for association journals, the law provides that there may be implied licenses granted to the association publishers. When a nonemployee submits an article for publication, for example, the publisher is deemed to have acquired the rights to reproduce and distribute the article in the particular collective work (e.g., an issue of a journal), in any revision of that work, and in any later collective work in the same series. The implied license does *not*, however, permit the association to publicly display or perform the article, nor to create a "derivative work," such as a book based upon the article.

If an association owns the copyright with respect to a given work, it can take affirmative steps to enhance its rights. It is not necessary for the association to affix a copyright notice to the work nor to register it with the government in order to be deemed the copyright owner; nevertheless, notice and registration play a vital role in the enhancement of a copyright owner's rights.

8. **Notice.** Placement of an appropriate copyright notice on a work will effectively preclude a copyright infringer from claiming "innocent infringement" and reducing liability exposure for the infringement. For most kinds of copyrightable works, the notice consists of the following three elements: (a) the letter c in a circle or the word *Copyright* (or both), (b) the year of the work's first "publication" (i.e., the year in which the work first was distributed to the public or offered for public distribution), and (c) the name of the copyright owner. (For audio recordings, known as "phonorecords" in the Copyright Act, the first element consists of a p in a circle rather than a c.)

9. **Registration.** Registration with the U.S. Copyright Office further enhances a copyright owner's interests. If the registration is accomplished before an act of copyright infringement occurs, the copyright owner may be able to recover increased damages for infringement. Registration may also entitle the copyright owner to recover costs and attorney's fees connected with enforcing the copyright.

10. **Use of works of others.** If an association were to make unauthorized use of copyrighted material owned by another party, it would risk violating the copyright laws and subjecting itself to suit for infringement. Because the exploitation of works protected by copyright can be profitable, and infringement can jeopardize those profits, copyright owners often are vigilant in enforcing their rights. Accordingly, engaging in the reproduction, distribution, or other use of works created by others carries some risk of copyright infringement. Even the performance of live or recorded music at an association's functions often involves the use of copyrighted works of others (and, unless the use of such music can be avoided or "public domain" music such as classical compositions can be used, "blanket" licenses for use of the repertories of the major performing rights organizations—ASCAP and BMI—must ordinarily be obtained). Some use of the work of others is absolutely essential, of course. When an association publishes or otherwise disseminates materials created by others, even with the permission of those persons, the association may not be aware that the creators of those materials have "borrowed" the contents from others (deliberately or inadvertently). These and many other situations raise potential copyright infringement liability risks for an association.

11. **Avoiding infringement.** In order to minimize the risk of copyright infringement liability exposure, responsible volunteers and staff of an association must learn about the sources of any works that the association publishes. If the association wishes to exercise one of the exclusive rights protected by copyright (e.g., reproduction, distribution, public performance), the association should determine whether the work in question is protected by copyright. Of course, if the work itself bears a copyright notice, there is at least some evidence of

copyright ownership. Works first published more than 75 years ago are not protected by copyright, although original arrangements of public domain works are protectable (e.g., a modern jazz version of a Bach fugue).

If a work is protected by copyright, the association has several options. First, it may simply choose not to use the work. Second, it may seek to obtain permission from the copyright owner (i.e., a license) for the intended use. Obviously, the license terms are negotiable, and it is possible that the copyright owner may refuse to grant the requested permission. Finally, in some circumstances, the association will be able to use the work without even seeking the copyright owner's permission because such use would constitute a "fair use" under federal copyright law.

12. **The "fair use" doctrine.** The "fair use" doctrine represents the law's attempt to balance the copyright owner's right to refuse permission for others to use a work against certain societal values rooted in the First Amendment—criticism, comment, news reporting, teaching, scholarship, and research. If use of a copyrighted work is "fair," then it does not infringe the copyright. The following four factors determine whether a particular use is fair:

a. the purpose and character of the use, including whether such use is of a commercial nature or is for nonprofit educational purposes;

b. the nature of the copyrighted work;

c. the amount and substantiality of the portion used in relation to the copyrighted work as a whole; and

d. the effect of the use upon the potential market for, or value of, the copyrighted work.

An association's nonprofit status will not excuse acts that otherwise would constitute clear copyright infringement, but in many instances, an association will be entitled to make limited use of copyrighted works because of the totality of the relevant factors involved in a given situation.

13. **Publication or republication of the works of others.** An association's regular use of works created by third parties (e.g., articles submitted by members for publication in the association's journals) raises additional potential for copyright infringement liability. The association should seek appropriate representations and warranties (and, in some circumstances, indemnification) from all third parties responsible for creating copyrightable works that the association will use. The representations and warranties should address the originality of the work, the author's role as its sole creator and owner, and the fact that the work does not violate any copyright interests or proprietary or personal rights of others.

Hypothetical Copyright Scenarios

The following scenarios illustrate the association's role as both a copyright owner and a potential copyright infringer. Any resemblance to actual fact situations or to real people or entities is unintentional.

Example 1: The Importance of Warranties

A committee of a national trade association decides to develop a "White Paper" on an important current product safety issue, with the lead in the effort to be taken by one of the committee members. The committee member adopts verbatim, and without attribution, language from two 5-page sections of a recently published article authored by someone else outside the association. The paper goes through several drafts over a period of months, and the committee member who was responsible for the initial draft is no longer on the committee when the paper is released. The association publishes the White Paper with some fanfare and is promptly sued by the publisher and the author of the original article from which the two segments were adapted. The association loses the suit and has no recourse against the committee member because the association failed to obtain a warranty from the member that the first draft of the White Paper was original and that it did not infringe on the works of third parties.

Example 2: Plagiarism

A professional association decides to publish a brochure for circulation by members to their clients about practice issues in the profession. It forms a committee to draft the brochure, and the members of the committee identify four existing publications in this area for reference. These publications are "cut and pasted" to produce the association's brochure, using the best elements of each, but no more than 500 words are taken from any one of the source publications. The total length of the association's brochure is 1,700 words. The association sells copies of the new brochure in bulk to members for a fee of $25 per 100 copies. The association is sued by the copyright owner of one of the source publications, who determines that 28% of the association's brochure is directly lifted or paraphrased from its own work. The association argues that its cut-and-paste work is fair use but loses. The court concludes that, despite the nonprofit, educational use of the association's brochure, it too greatly reduced the value of this source publication, from which it was in part assembled.

Example 3: Association Committee Work

A committee of an association in the banking industry is commissioned by the association's board to produce a how-to book on customer service. Each member of the committee agrees to write a particular chapter of the book, and an association staff member coordinates the project (but does none of the writing). The book is published and is a great success within the industry; it becomes recognized as the "bible" for banks on customer service. Two years later, the association staff, drawing on the success of the book, engages an outside firm to create a 30-minute videotape derived from the central chapter of the book, on general principles of customer service. Staff does not obtain a further license or assignment of copyright from the chapter's author.

The chapter author makes a claim against the association for copyright infringement and prevails; the association pays a substantial settlement award based on the revenues from the videotape. The association was not the initial copyright owner, nor was there any written assignment of the chapter to the association. It clearly had a license to reproduce the chapter created by the author, but its rights were limited to the book in question and to any later books in the series; they did not include rights to adapt the chapter into a videotape. The association should have taken steps to ensure that its rights extended to other uses of the chapter.

Example 4: Fair Use

A busy and highly respected member of an association of accountants writes an article for a commercially published national professional journal. The article is extremely well received within the profession and is sought by the association's staff for reproduction in conjunction with an educational program on the same subject. The association staff contacts the article's author and requests permission for the reproduction. The author is flattered and grants the consent. Unfortunately, the author does not recall that one of the "standard forms" that was required of authors by the journal included a copyright assignment in favor of the journal's publisher. The journal regularly allows requesting parties to obtain article reprints for a specified fee. The registration charge for attendees at the association's educational program is $300; those who are unable to attend but wish to receive the program materials are charged $150.

The scientific journal publisher learns of the unauthorized use of the article and sues the association. The association argues that its use was protected under the fair use doctrine but loses this argument. The court notes that the association had appropriated the entire article, not just a portion of it, and that the publisher would have been entitled to reprint revenues. The association pays nominal damages and is required to pay the publisher's attorney's fees and costs (as well as its own), because the journal issue was registered with the U.S. Copyright Office prior to the infringement.

When an association obtains authorization for the use of copyrighted materials, it should take steps to ensure that whoever provides the authorization has permission from the actual copyright owner to provide it.

Example 5: The Association as Plaintiff

An association's publications department commissions and publishes another how-to book like that cited in Example 1. This time, the department is careful to secure written copyright assignments from each of the chapter authors and has affixed an appropriate copyright notice on each copy of the published book. It does not register the work with the U.S. Copyright Office, however. One year later, the association discovers that a textbook publisher has, without permission, paraphrased or copied verbatim substantial portions of the association's book. Although the textbook has become the leader in its field and is used by thousands of students each year, the textbook publisher has actually lost money in this venture.

The association registers its copyright interest with the U.S. Copyright Office and sues the textbook publisher for copyright infringement. The court finds that the textbook publisher has infringed the association's copyright, but the association is able to recover only minimal damages and no attorney's fees because it failed to register the work before the infringement. The fees that the association pays to trial counsel actually exceed the recovered damages; the association does, however, obtain an injunction against further use of the material.

If the work had been registered promptly upon publication, the outcome of this litigation would have been far better for the association.

How Does One Maximize the Association's Rights and Minimize Its Risk?

1.   Before exercising one or more of the rights subsumed under copyright, an association should satisfy itself that it is legally entitled to exercise those rights, either as a copyright owner or licensee under the fair use doctrine or under another of the statutory limitations on copyright.
2.   The association should affix appropriate copyright notices to all copies and recordings of association works.
3.   The association should at least consider copyright registration with respect to those works in which it owns the copyright; association clerical staff can easily file the registrations. Where appropriate, registration should be accomplished within 3 months after first publication.
4.   The association should seek written copyright assignments or licenses from nonemployees responsible for creating copyrightable works that the association will publish or sell. Although the terms of any assignment or license will depend upon the specific facts involved, the association always should seek appropriate representations and warranties to protect itself against liability for infringement of the interests of third parties.
5.   The association should not assume that its exercise of any of the rights subsumed under a copyright constitutes fair use until it has thoroughly analyzed all of the fair use factors.
6.   The association should bear in mind that copyright law differs from country to country. The material in this chapter is applicable to works created by U.S. nationals or domiciliaries, works first published in the United States, and other works subject to the jurisdiction of the federal copyright statute by its terms. The copyright laws of other countries may come into play when the association seeks to use the works of foreign authors or when it publishes or distributes works abroad.

Part VI

Legal Issues in Employment

Introduction

The two chapters in Part VI discuss legal concerns that affect every trade or professional association that has employees. Chapter 19 covers employment discrimination, a subject that must be understood by all association supervising employees or even volunteers that have responsibility for dealing with employment matters. Chapter 20 covers wrongful discharge, an area of legal liability for associations and all employers that is of increasing importance. This chapter helps educate association leadership regarding the right ways to terminate employment when such action becomes necessary.

19

Employment Discrimination

What Is Employment Discrimination?

Under various federal antidiscrimination statutes, associations and other employers are prohibited from discriminating against employees in hiring; discharge; compensation; promotion; classification; training; apprenticeship; referral for employment; and other terms, conditions and privileges of employment on the basis of race, color, sex (including pregnancy), age, national origin, religion, and physical or mental disability. In addition, there are many state and local antidiscrimination statutes that prohibit employment discrimination based on various other factors, including marital status, sexual orientation, and medical status. There is also the phenomenon of "reverse discrimination," where the association employer can be accused of unfairly favoring protected classes of employees to the detriment of nonprotected classes. Every association should have a strict policy to avoid all forms of unlawful employment discrimination.

Intent to discriminate is not required to establish a cause of action for employment discrimination. Neutral employment policies that have a "disparate impact" on members of one of the protected groups can form the basis for a discrimination suit against an association. In addition, the association will generally be liable for the discriminatory conduct of its employee supervisors, volunteers who take a role in employment matters, and others in authority.

Who Is at Risk for Employment Discrimination in an Association?

Every association that is an employer is at risk for employment discrimination liability every time it or one of its supervisors, volunteers, or other representatives makes an employment decision. Based on the damages provisions of the Civil Rights Act of 1991, which provide for compensatory and punitive damages for violations of various antidiscrimination statutes, employment discrimination can result in substantial liability for an association and, in some circumstances, for the individual supervisor involved.

What Are the Main Principles of Employment Discrimination?

The law of employment discrimination is complex, not always entirely intuitive, and can vary in some circumstances from state to state. The following are the main principles in this area for association employee/supervisors, and any volunteers who deal in employment matters, to keep in mind.

1. **Race discrimination.** Title VII of the Civil Rights Act of 1964 prohibits discrimination in all aspects of the employment relationship based on race or color. White individuals as well as racial minorities can have a cause of action under Title VII if they are discriminated against on the basis of race.

2. **Sex discrimination.** Title VII prohibits discrimination in employment also on the basis of sex. Both men and women can bring Title VII actions for sex discrimination.

   a. *Pregnancy discrimination.* Sex discrimination includes discrimination on the basis of pregnancy. A pregnant employee must be treated in the same way as any other employee, and when a female employee becomes unable to work due to pregnancy, childbirth, or related medical conditions, her disability must be treated the same as any other disability. An association's medical insurance plan may not exclude coverage for pregnancies. In addition, child care leave (as distinguished from pregnancy disability leave) must be provided to men and women on an equal basis.

   b. *Sexual harassment.* Sexual harassment is also part of the unlawful sex discrimination forbidden by Title VII. The federal Equal Employment Opportunity Commission (EEOC) has defined sexual harassment as "unwelcome sexual advances, requests for sexual favors, and other verbal or physical conduct of a sexual nature." Requests, advances, or conduct of this kind constitute sexual harassment when: (i) it is an employment condition, that is, submission to the conduct is made a term or condition of employment; (ii) it is an employment consequence, that is, submission to, or rejection of, the conduct is used as a basis for employment decisions affecting the individual; or (iii) it is an offensive job interference, that is, the conduct has the purpose or effect of unreasonably interfering with an employee's work performance or creating an intimidating, hostile, or offensive working environment.

   An association is generally liable for harassment by supervisors. In addition, the association could be held liable for hostile environment harassment by co-employees or nonemployees if those in charge at the association knew, or should have known, of the harassment and did not take immediate steps to correct the problem. Those responsible for harassment may also be personally liable.

3. **Religious discrimination.** Title VII prohibits employment discrimination on the basis of an individual's religious belief. "Traditional" religions and religious beliefs are not the only beliefs covered by Title VII. The EEOC defines "religious practices" to include "moral or ethical beliefs as to what is right or wrong, which are sincerely held with the strength of traditional religious views." In addition, the absence of religious beliefs is included in the definition of religion; so employ-

ment discrimination based upon an individual's absence of religious beliefs is also prohibited.

An association employer must make "reasonable accommodation" to the religious practices of employees and applicants. Accommodation is not required, however, if it causes "undue hardship" to the employer. An employer is not required to bear more than a *de minimis* cost in accommodating an employee's religious beliefs and is not required to discriminate against other employees.

4. **Disability discrimination.** The Americans with Disabilities Act (ADA) requires associations and other employers to make "reasonable accommodations" to the known physical or mental limitations of otherwise qualified disabled individuals unless to do so would impose "undue hardship" on the employers' operations. The standard for requiring reasonable accommodation under the ADA is much more stringent than the standard for religious accommodation discussed earlier. The ADA requires an employer to accommodate a disabled employee, absent significant difficulty or expense.

5. **Age discrimination.** The Age Discrimination in Employment Act (ADEA) prohibits discrimination on the basis of age against employees age 40 or older. The ADEA also prohibits discriminating on the basis of age between two individuals, both of whom are over age 40. An association or other employer may not discriminate on the basis of age with regard to hiring, discharge, compensation, or other terms or conditions of employment.

6. **National origin discrimination.** Title VII prohibits employment discrimination on the basis of national origin. National origin has been broadly defined as the country from which an applicant or employee, or his or her forbears, came.

Hypothetical Scenarios on Employment Discrimination

The following scenarios illustrate the legal risks and principles of selected employment discrimination issues. Any resemblance to actual persons or existing entities is completely unintentional.

Example 1: Religious Discrimination

An association hires an employee whose religion does not allow him to work on Sundays. Occasionally, however, the position requires that the individual work on Sundays, such as at the association's annual convention or at other meetings and educational events. The employee informs his supervisor that he will not be able to work on any Sundays. The supervisor informs him that he is required to work at an upcoming annual convention and offers to provide a paid "comp" day off for the employee in view of the Sunday work. When the employee does not report to work on the Sunday of the convention, he is terminated. The employee sues the association for religious discrimination under Title VII. The court holds the association liable, finding that it did not attempt to reasonably accommodate the religious practices of the employee. The association is liable to the employee for compensation and punitive damages, as well as for appropriate equitable relief such as reinstatement and back pay.

Example 2: Sexual Harassment

A supervisor of a large association's education and meeting planning department is a longtime association employee. The department is large and successful, and the supervisor is regarded by senior association staff and the volunteer leaders to be an excellent manager.

The supervisor holds weekly staff meetings. During these meetings, the supervisor routinely uses crude language and tells jokes that some of the employees consider "off-color" and "of a suggestive sexual nature." The supervisor also winks at staff while talking to them, makes comments about staff members' appearance (how they are dressed, their pleasant smile, comments on perfume/aftershave, etc.). This conduct has been perceived as unwelcome by several staff members. Some of the staff have complained among themselves and to peers outside of the department about the supervisor's conduct. There have also been complaints to the association's human resources department, which do not get reported to the association's senior executives.

The education and meeting planning department supervisor's secretary, when discussing this conduct with others, typically characterizes the supervisor as charming and harmless, albeit a bit "flirtatious." Two new employees in the department are particularly surprised by the general acceptance of the conduct and mention their concern to the supervisor's secretary, who reports their comment at lunch one day to the supervisor. A few days later, they are upset because they feel they were given more work and higher production requirements than employees at a similar level. They approach the supervisor and ask why their work has increased. They are told, "I'm the boss, and if you're so serious about your job and can't joke around with me like the others do, you'd better look somewhere else."

The employees are confused about the proper internal steps to take, so they decide to file a charge with the EEOC. The EEOC investigates and determines that sexual harassment has occurred. It bases this determination on the fact that so many employees find the supervisor's conduct offensive and on the fact that when the supervisor learned of the complaints, there was apparently retaliation against the employees who complained. The association's leadership never learned about the harassment, but the association is nevertheless held liable because the supervisor's retaliation converted the harassment from "hostile environment" harassment to quid pro quo harassment, for which the association is strictly liable.

How Can an Association Minimize Its Risk of Employment Discrimination Claims?

1. Closely review employment applications and remove any unlawful inquiries. Be particularly mindful of the requirements of the ADA,

and be certain to eliminate any questions inquiring about physical or mental limitations that do not relate to an applicant's ability to perform the job.

2. Properly train all individuals involved in the hiring process concerning the "do's" and "don'ts," from an equal employment perspective, in dealing with preemployment inquiries.

3. Review proposed position requirements and make certain that each of the job requirements is job-related to avoid any potential claim that the job qualifications are exclusionary or discriminatory in nature.

4. Ensure that all equal employment notices are properly posted as required by law.

5. Audit applicant flow, hiring, promotion, and termination decisions to ensure the absence of discrimination.

6. Carefully audit compliance with the ADA, including making reasonable accommodations to qualified individuals with disabilities; note that the administration of tests that relate to professional credentials carry special ADA requirements.

7. Maintain properly drafted equal employment and sexual harassment policies, including an internal complaint procedure to deal with claims. Periodically reaffirm the policies through newsletters, postings, and other communications with employees.

8. Train supervisors to be sensitive to equal employment issues. Advise them that any discriminatory conduct or statements will not be tolerated in any circumstances.

9. Promptly investigate any complaint of sexual harassment or other employment-related discrimination and take appropriate steps to immediately correct problems.

10. In dealing with problem employees, be certain to prepare proper documentation to support any association action, including documenting meetings with the employee. Remember that this documentation may be a critical means of refreshing recollection in the event of a challenge.

11. Ensure that an independent review is made of all proposed termination decisions.

12. Consider establishing a meaningful employee complaint procedure, including evaluating whether a formal alternative dispute resolution mechanism, such as mediation and/or arbitration, is warranted.

13. Closely monitor, with the assistance of counsel, developments at the local, state, and federal level to ensure compliance with changing equal employment requirements.

20 _____

Wrongful Discharge

What Is Wrongful Discharge?

An employee may bring a wrongful discharge action against the employer for discharging the employee in violation of the law. A wrongful discharge action is generally based on an exception to the "employment-at-will" doctrine and may be brought under either contract or tort theories of law.

The general rule in American law is that employees who are hired for an indefinite period of time are "employees-at-will." This means that an employee may be terminated by the employer at any time for any reason or for no reason. Similarly, the employee may voluntarily terminate employment at any time. Although this remains the general rule, various exceptions have been imposed over time. It is important for an association/employer to be aware of these exceptions, because wrongful discharge cases based on the exceptions to the employment-at-will doctrine have increased dramatically in recent years.

Who Is at Risk for Wrongful Discharge?

As an employer, any association is at risk for a wrongful discharge claim any time it discharges an employee. Notwithstanding, an association can minimize the risks from wrongful discharge claims if it properly understands the various exceptions to the employment-at-will doctrine.

What Legal Principles Have Been Applied?

Tort theories hold wrongdoers responsible for personal injury or property damage. Several tort theories have been carved out as exceptions to the employment-at-will doctrine.

1. **Violation of public policy.** Many statutes prohibit employers from discharging employees in retaliation for the employees' exercising their rights under the statute. In addition, even if there are not specific statutory provisions, many states allow an employee to recover damages for a discharge that contravenes the public policy of the state. In many states, it is unlawful to discharge an employee in retaliation for some or all of the following reasons: (a) refusing to commit an unlawful act; (b) performing an important public obligation (e.g., reporting for jury duty); (c) exercising a legal right established by statute or case

law (e.g., claiming workers compensation benefits, refusing to take a polygraph test where the test is statutorily prohibited, retaining a lawyer to negotiate a wage claim with the employer); and (d) "whistle-blowing" (i.e., reporting an employer's unlawful acts).

Because each state recognizes different public policy exceptions, an association should seek legal advice prior to discharging an employee who has engaged in any of these potentially protected activities.

2. **Implied covenant of good faith and fair dealing.** A very limited number of states have implied a covenant, or promise, of good faith and fair dealing into every contract, including employment "contracts" otherwise terminable at will. Under this theory, an employer may be held liable for failing to exercise good faith in terminating an at-will employee. Generally, however, even states that recognize this exception to employment-at-will limit recovery under the theory. For example, California, which is one of the few states to even recognize this cause of action, has disallowed compensatory and punitive damages for violations of the implied covenant of good faith and fair dealing.

In contrast to tort theories, contract theories hold wrongdoers liable for breaching a contract or breaking a promise. The following contract theories have been applied as exceptions to the employment-at-will doctrine.

1. **Express employment contract.** An actual written contract for employment, which provides for a specific time period of employment or for discharge only for specific reasons or only for just cause obviously alters the employment-at-will relationship. In the case where an employee has such an employment contract, the association employer must follow the specific contract provisions. In addition, the vast majority of collective bargaining agreements contain provisions that allow employers to discharge employees only for just cause, thus altering the employment-at-will relationship.

2. **Explicit "just cause" provisions.** Oral or written statements that employees will be terminated only for just cause have been found sufficient to create an enforceable promise, even if the employment relationship is for an indefinite term. It should be noted that any ambiguities in personnel policies will typically be construed against the employer.

3. **Implicit "just cause" provisions.** Courts themselves have also implied just cause provisions in a number of different circumstances. These circumstances include personnel policies, handbooks, or disciplinary guidelines that outline specific actions that will lead to discharge and that distinguish between probationary and nonprobationary employees. Also included are oral assurances that an employee will have a job as long the employee does good work. Various courts have found implied just cause provisions in these circumstances because employees could reasonably believe that their employers would

discharge them only for cause (such as only for the reasons specifically discussed in the employee handbook).

4. **Disclaimers.** Because an employee's reasonable reliance is essential to establishing just cause limitations on the employment-at-will relationship, disclaimers in handbooks and other personnel policies and employment applications can remove or avoid "just cause" job protections. A disclaimer that is clearly communicated to employees in an authorized, published writing may help rebut an employee's contention of reasonable reliance on implied just cause provisions.

Hypothetical Scenarios

These scenarios illustrate some of the legal risks and principles of wrongful discharge. Any resemblance to actual persons or existing entities is completely unintentional.

Example 1: Public Policy Exception

An association's annual meeting is approaching; due to the heavy workload, the chief executive officer (CEO) asks all employees to refrain from taking time off during normal working hours to vote in a local election. The local law provides that employers must provide notice to employees of the opportunity to take reasonable paid leave to vote. One employee refuses to comply with the CEO's request, stating that the law gives employees a right to paid leave. The employee is soon terminated, in part for what is termed "insubordination." The employee then brings a wrongful discharge lawsuit against the association, alleging that the termination violated the public policy of the local jurisdiction.

The association, which does not dispute the facts alleged by the employee but argues that there were other sound reasons for the termination besides "insubordination" in connection with the employee's taking leave time to vote, loses the suit on the employee's summary judgment motion. The court finds that the association violated the public policy of the local jurisdiction by refusing to permit paid leave time for voting. The Court awards the employee punitive damages in the amount of $50,000 to discourage the association from repeating its conduct.

Associations should not terminate employees for reasons that conflict with public policy.

Example 2: Implied Contract

A large state association distributes an employee handbook that contains a "progressive" disciplinary procedure that states:

> Beginning ninety days after each employee's starting date, employment becomes permanent; termination by the association will not occur without proper notice and investigation. Permanent employees receive prior written

admonitions before termination. Three warnings within a twelve-month period are required before an employee is dismissed, except in the case of grave offenses that warrant immediate dismissal. [Examples of grave offenses are listed.]

The handbook does not contain any disclaimers of contractual intent. Subsequently, the association dismisses an employee for failure to follow association procedures (not an enumerated grave offense) without giving prior written warnings.

The employee brings suit against the association for breach of an employment contract for failure to follow the disciplinary procedures set forth in the employee handbook. The association loses the suit. The court finds an implied contract created by the employee handbook. The court holds that the employee handbook constituted an offer to the employee of its terms, and, by continuing to work under the terms set forth in the handbook, the employee accepted the terms. This offer and acceptance created an enforceable contract. The court awards the employee contract damages in the form of lost wages and other employment benefits.

An association employer should consider carefully the ramifications of all features of its employment policies and then must adhere strictly to those policies.

Example 3: Implied Contract

Same facts as above, except the handbook contains a disclaimer, laid out in bold print on the first page of the handbook, that states:

> This handbook is intended only for your information and guidance. It is not an employment contract and does not guarantee any fixed terms or conditions. It should be regarded as merely guidelines on the requirements and procedures of employment; management reserves the right to alter those procedures at any time without prior notice. Employment with the association is for no definite period and is terminable at will.

This time, the association wins the suit. The court holds that the disclaimer effectively supersedes any implied contract created by the disciplinary procedures.

Example 4: Verbal Contract

A national professional association is extremely interested in hiring a particular applicant for employment, whose unique technical credentials would be very useful in providing services to the membership. During the course of recruiting, the applicant asks one of the association interviewers about job security at the association. The interviewer states that "you will be with the association as long as you do your job." The interviewer further states that the applicant would never have to look for another job because the interviewer knew of no one that the association had ever terminated.

The applicant accepts the position. Several years later, the applicant is terminated. In a wrongful discharge suit against the association for breach of an employment agreement only to terminate for just cause, the employee proves that the statements of job security were indeed made at the time of employment (the original association interviewer who made the statements has long left the association but remained friendly to the plaintiff in the suit). The association attempts to obtain an early dismissal of the case, but the court holds that the terminated employee can maintain the cause of action against the association because the interviewer's statements regarding job security created an enforceable employment contract to terminate only for cause. A jury finds that the association did not terminate the employee for cause and awards back pay for the association's breach of the employment contract.

How Does One Minimize Risk to the Association From Wrongful Discharge Claims?

Although nothing an association employer does can prevent terminated employees from filing claims of wrongful discharge, some guidelines will help associations to defend against the claims.

1. In making discharge decisions, never discriminate on the basis of race, sex, religion, national origin, age, disability, marital status, or sexual orientation. (See chap. 19, "Employment Discrimination.")
2. In making discharge decisions, avoid public policy problems. If the employee recently has exercised a legal right relating to the workplace, been involved in any controversial events involving alleged misconduct by the association, refused to commit an unlawful act, or performed an important public obligation, obtain legal advice prior to terminating the employee.
3. Review employee handbooks and avoid creating contract language in written policies. Include disclaimer language in the introduction to the handbooks. Be certain the disclaimer is "clear and conspicuous."
4. In any termination or "progressive" discipline policy, (a) include disclaimers, (b) reserve employer discretion, and (c) make certain the policy is realistic.
5. Educate employment interviewers to avoid "puffing." In other words, in attempting to recruit a desired applicant, do not make misleading promises of employment security.
6. Adopt proper work rules or employee standards of conduct and follow them. A disclaimer of contractual intent should be included in work rules or employee standards of conduct.
7. Performance appraisals should be realistic. Regular and realistic assessments of an employee's performance will minimize the risk that

an employee can successfully accuse the employer of unfair treatment.

8. Establish uniform discipline and counseling guidelines.
9. Give special consideration to long-term employees.
10. Consider establishing an internal grievance procedure. Include a disclaimer of contractual intent in the procedure.
11. Ensure that there is an independent review of all termination decisions.
12. All written employment contracts should be carefully drafted with respect to termination and should be reviewed by association counsel before execution.

Appendix A   ————————————

Sample Conflicts of Interest Policy

Background

Under the law, all volunteers of trade and professional associations, such as members of association boards, committees, or other governing bodies, owe a *duty of care* and a *duty of loyalty* to their associations. Even though they serve as unpaid volunteers, individuals who hold positions in these bodies can be held *legally liable* to the association—and the association can likewise be held legally liable to others—if these duties of care or loyalty are violated and damages result. Avoidance of conflicts of interest is also an obligation of association employees.

Briefly stated, volunteers and employees must always *act reasonably and in the best interests of the association*; they must *avoid negligence and fraud* in performing their activities on behalf of the association; and they must *avoid conflicts of interest* between their duties to the association and their duties to other organizations.

Volunteers and employees owe the association their undivided allegiance. *A conflict of interest exists when an individual participates in the deliberation and resolution of an issue important to the association while, at the same time, the individual has other professional, business, or volunteer responsibilities outside the association that could predispose or bias the individual to a particular view or goal.*

There are three ways to avoid legal liability for volunteers and employees, as well as for the association, arising from conflicts of interest. For serious and actual conflicts, the individual must *voluntarily withdraw*—or be withdrawn involuntarily if necessary—from the association position. For less serious conflicts, there must be *disclosure to the association and avoidance of participating* in debate and voting on the issue for which there is a conflict (known as *recusal*). Finally, for only minor or potential conflicts, there must be *full disclosure* to the association.

Only judgment and experience can determine which kind of conflict exists and therefore which resolution of the conflict is appropriate. Ultimately, it is the association's prerogative, not that of the individual, to make determinations regarding conflicts.

In any legal challenge, conflicts will be judged from the point of view of disinterested outsiders, so it is prudent to err on the conservative side and *avoid even the appearance of conflicts of interest.*

Examples

Example A

Assume that an individual sits on the governing board of an association's for-profit subsidiary, which conducts a fee-for-service consulting program for the field represented by the parent association; at the same time, the individual sits on the governing board of a business corporation in which the individual is called upon to make decisions regarding management of the corporation's own consulting program that competes directly with that of the association subsidiary. Here, the problem is that the individual has active responsibility for the management of two competing programs. This is the kind of extreme conflict that demands that the individual not serve on the association subsidiary's governing board.

Example B

Assume that a member of an association committee is a recognized technical expert in an area in which the committee plans to conduct a survey; after taking competing bids and assuring that it is paying a "market rate," the committee recommends that the association engage the individual at a reasonable compensation level to assist with the survey. Here, it would be adequate for there to be full disclosure to the committee and the association at the time of the engagement, as well as periodic reminders to the committee and the association later about the vendor relationship, plus avoidance of participation by the individual in discussing and resolving issues related to the area of the engagement (recusal).

Special care should always be taken, however, when an individual serving as an association volunteer is also a vendor, or an employee or consultant for a vendor, that provides products or services to the association or its members in any capacity. There must be meticulously complete and periodically repeated disclosure of those dual relationships, as well as avoidance of participation in debate and resolution of issues at the association related to the vendor situation.

Example C

Finally, assume that a member of an association's governing board is affiliated as an instructor at an educational institution that, among many other offerings, provides continuing education to those in the field represented by the association. The association itself, of course, also offers extensive educational programming in that field. Here, the individual is not actively managing an endeavor that directly competes with the association, so this is not a serious conflict situation. It would be wise, however, for the individual to disclose this outside relationship in general terms to colleagues at the association, although withdrawal or recusal would not be required.

Procedures

The following procedures are recommended to assist in avoiding conflicts of interest among association volunteers and employees:

1. Those responsible for nominating or appointing leaders to positions on association boards, committees, and other governing bodies, as well as those responsible for interviewing and hiring employees, should be alert for possible conflicts and should explore questionable situations thoroughly before making the nomination, appointment, or hiring decisions.

2. When conflicts or potential conflicts arise, they should be evaluated thoroughly, using the assistance of association legal counsel if necessary, and resolved appropriately.

3. Where individuals serving voluntarily on behalf of an association or as association employees are also engaged in a capacity as vendors to the association or its members, special attention should be given to ensure that the individuals provide full disclosure and avoid participation in related issues at the association.

4. Each year, volunteer members of boards, committees, and other governing bodies of the association, as well as association employees, should disclose to the association any situations or areas of actual or potential conflicts of interest. A form is attached to serve as a model for this purpose.

DISCLOSURE REGARDING CONFLICTS OF INTEREST

As a volunteer or employee of the association, I recognize that I owe duties of care and loyalty to the association. One aspect of fulfilling those duties is to avoid conflicts of interest in which my allegiance might be split between an association position or responsibility and some other professional, business, or volunteer position or responsibility. To help avoid conflicts, on this form I am disclosing other situations or areas in which it might even appear that I have conflicting duties to other entities. I invite any further review by the association of any aspects of these situations or areas that might be considered appropriate. Also, I will take other steps, such as avoiding deliberation and resolution of certain issues or even withdrawing from my position in the association, if it is determined that those steps are necessary to protect against legal liability to the association or to me arising from conflicts of interest.

1. Professional, business, or volunteer positions or responsibilities that might give rise to conflicts: _____

_____

_____

_____

_____

_____

_____

_____

2. Situations in which I am serving as a vendor, or am employed by or consulting with a vendor, to the association or its members: _____

_____

_____

_____

_____

3. I know of no professional, business, or volunteer position or responsibility, including vendor situations, that might give rise to conflicts (check here): _____.

_____   _____
Signature   Date

_____
Association position

Appendix B

Sample Guidelines on Apparent Authority

Introduction

In 1982, the United States Supreme Court determined that a professional association was liable for antitrust violations arising from activities of its volunteers or employees, even when the association and its leadership did not know about, approve of, or benefit from those activities, as long as the volunteers or employees appeared to outsiders to be acting with the association's approval (i.e., with its "apparent authority").

The famous decision is *American Society of Mechanical Engineers, Inc. v. Hydrolevel Corp.* In it, the Supreme Court established the principle potentially applicable to all trade and professional associations, of any size or kind, that associations are to be held strictly liable for the activities of volunteers and employees that have even the apparent authority of the associations. The imposition of liability is intended as a warning to associations that they must adopt and follow procedures to ensure that antitrust violations, even unauthorized ones, do not occur.

These Apparent Authority Guidelines provide guidance for volunteers and employees of associations on the limits of their authority to act on behalf of the associations.

The Apparent Authority Guidelines apply to all groups of volunteers and employees of an association, that is, councils, boards, divisions, committees, sections, subcommittees, ad hoc groups, task forces, work groups, and so on.

Guidelines

1. **Standards, guidelines, and credentials.** Extreme care is necessary in the development of standards, guidelines, or credentials that affect economic interests or competition. When these kinds of association programs might have effects upon (a) prices or terms of sale for products or services, areas or customer groups served, volume or availability of products or services, relationships with suppliers or customers, or other economic or competitive factors in a business or industry; or (b) fees, scope of practice or modes of practice, compensation or reimbursement, professional engagements or positions, assignment of tasks or titles, or other economic or competitive factors in a profession, then the antitrust laws are implicated.

Standards, guidelines, or credentials must be reasonable. Reasonableness can be enhanced by circulating the proposed standards, guidelines, or credentials for comment by those who will be affected. The final versions should reflect, to the extent practicable, the consensus of opinion of those affected by the standards, guidelines, or credentials after review and consideration of all comments received.

Standards, guidelines, and credentials must state who is authorized to interpret them. Interpretations should be issued in writing following legal review. Extreme care must be used in formulating any statements regarding standards, guidelines, or credentials that are expected to be relied upon by association members or by others, whether or not there are specific enforcement mechanisms related to the standards, guidelines, or credentials.

If the standards, guidelines, or credentials do include enforcement mechanisms, there must be provisions to ensure that due process is afforded to those affected, including the opportunity for appeal.

2. **Correspondence and statements.** Official correspondence and statements, whether issued explicitly or implicitly by or on behalf of an association, must be approved in advance.

Approval can be either by the entire body responsible for the correspondence or statements, such as where the association's governing board or a committee has voted on a resolution to issue correspondence or statements, or by the highest level of volunteer leadership or employed leadership involved, such as the chair of the board or committee or the chief staff official responsible for the board or committee, if the body has delegated authority to those individuals. The correspondence or statements must then be limited to what has been authorized and must be within the scope of the duties of the volunteer or employed leadership.

Other correspondence or statements must not be on association letterhead and, if they could possibly be interpreted as issued by or on behalf of the association, must include a disclaimer indicating that they are not made by or on behalf of the association.

3. **Meetings and conflicts.** All association meetings must be scheduled in advance if practicable, have agendas circulated to attendees in advance, be open if practicable, and have written minutes prepared and circulated to attendees.

Questions and Answers on the "Apparent Authority Guidelines"

1. To whom do the Guidelines apply?

The Guidelines are intended to protect the association from acts that incur legal liability for activities of association volunteers or staff who may appear to third parties to be speaking or acting with real or apparent authority on any matter. Therefore, they apply to all association volunteers or employees who might take action or make statements that carry or appear to carry the authority of the association. This includes association officers; directors; board, committee, subcommittee, task force, or ad hoc group chairs and members; and any others in leadership positions in the association's governance structure. Finally, it includes all association employees.

2. The Apparent Authority Guidelines apply specially to "standards, guidelines, and credentials"; how are these identified?

Standards include any criteria, protocols, or specifications for conduct, performance, services, or products in the field represented by the association or in other fields. Included are both required and recommended standards, because government authorities have said that the recommendations of an association might have a "chilling effect" on members or others who might otherwise act contrary to a recommendation. Guidelines likewise include pronouncements, statements, or declarations that suggest or recommend specific activities, behavior, endeavors, or conduct for association members. As with standards, concern is warranted with respect to guidelines whether or not any enforcement mechanism is applicable. Credentials include any criteria or requirements that are conditions for obtaining use of titles, logos, seals, designations, memberships, or membership classes. Whenever safety, quality, competence, experience, or education are reviewed, credentialing likely occurs. Of particular concern are standards, guidelines, and credentials that affect economic interests or competition, because the law prohibits unreasonable criteria and inadequate procedures in those cases.

3. How is "consensus" achieved for standards, guidelines, or credentials?

The concept of consensus in developing, interpreting, or enforcing a program of standards, guidelines, or credentials includes a sincere attempt to obtain the views of all who will be affected by the program, both inside and outside of the association, and careful consideration of those views; it does not require unanimity of support as long as dissenters' views have been considered and rejected for valid reasons not related to economic interests or competition. The essentials of consensus building are distribution of proposals among those who will be significantly affected, solicitation of their comments, and careful consideration of those comments. It is desirable to document and retain documentation of the circulation of proposals and consideration of any comments.

4. What "due process" is required in programs of standards, guidelines, or credentials?

Associations, since they are private, nongovernmental entities, are not required to follow the complex procedures of governmental agencies. However, when dealing with standards, guidelines, or credentials that affect economic interests or competition, associations may be regarded as "quasigovernmental." They should provide at least the basic elements of due process. In most cases, this includes notice to one who may be affected by an adverse decision, opportunity to challenge the decision, including possibly at an informal hearing, and appeal to some body other than the body that made the original adverse decision.

5. Who should have routine access to association letterhead?

In most cases, only association employees should have routine access to the association's letterhead, because employees should be involved in preparing or reviewing all official correspondence.

6. Are emergency meetings precluded by these Guidelines?

No. Routine meetings should be scheduled in advance with notice and the agenda distributed to attendees. However, there may well be need for emergency meetings. In those cases, there should at least be minutes prepared and distributed to attendees.

7. Can private meetings be held, such as to evaluate association employees?

Yes. There should not be "secret" or clandestine meetings of any association body. However, there may be legitimate reasons to meet in executive session or otherwise to preserve confidentiality of discussions at meetings. Evaluation of association employees is likely such a reason. Meetings, or portions of meetings, held in executive session should be carefully limited, because the mere fact of confidentiality will by itself spur the interest of investigators and challengers if government or private legal investigations or challenges arise.

Appendix C _____

Sample Antitrust Compliance Policy

This association has a policy of strict compliance with the nation's antitrust laws. The antitrust laws prohibit agreements among competitors, and association members can be considered competitors in the context of antitrust challenges even if their businesses (or professional practices) are not in the same geographic areas or in the same product lines (or professional fields or specialties). The penalties for violations of the antitrust laws can be very severe—not only for the association but also for its members. These laws were intended to protect smaller competitors from unfair practices of larger competitors. For example, suppliers are prohibited by the antitrust laws from engaging in collective action against customers or users. This association and its members have a corresponding obligation to strictly obey the antitrust laws themselves.

Members of the association cannot come to understandings, make agreements, or otherwise concur on positions or activities that in any way tend to raise, lower, or stabilize prices (or fees), divide up markets, or encourage boycotts. Each member must decide for itself, without consultation with competitors, how to conduct its business (or its professional practice) and with whom to do business (or engage in professional practice). Specifically, members should not agree on:

- Current or future prices (or fees), price (or fee) changes, discounting, and other terms and conditions of sale (or of providing professional services). Members should be extremely careful about discussing prices (or fees). Agreements on pricing (or fees) are clearly illegal. Even price (or fee) discussions by competitors, if followed by parallel decisions on pricing (or fees), can lead to antitrust investigations or challenges.
- Allocating territories or customers (or patients, clients, etc.). Any agreement by competitors to "honor," "protect," or "avoid invading" one another's market areas or product lines (or professional practice areas) would violate the law.
- Refusing to do business with those whose business practices they oppose. Competitors can discuss the policies or practices of suppliers (or reimbursers), but they must never threaten directly or indirectly to act jointly to enforce changes to those policies or practices. Again, discussions followed by parallel decision making could at least trigger careful antitrust scrutiny.

Discussions of pricing (or fees) or boycotts as part of association-scheduled programming or at association-sponsored meetings could implicate and involve the association in extensive and expensive antitrust challenges. The U.S. Supreme Court has determined that recommendations or exhortations in antitrust areas by individuals who might appear to represent an association in some capacity can likewise jeopardize the association, so those in positions of responsibility for the association must be especially cautious.

The antitrust laws are complicated and often unclear. If any member is concerned that he or she may be in a "gray area," that member should consult with the association's senior executives or legal counsel. If the conversation among competitors at an association meeting turns to antitrust-sensitive issues, participants should discontinue the conversation until legal advice is obtained, or else leave the meeting immediately.

Index

About the Authors

Jerald A. Jacobs is a partner of the Jenner & Block law firm and resident in its Washington office. He is head of the firm's Association Practice Group, which provides counseling and advocacy for over 250 national trade and professional associations. Jacobs received his AB, cum laude, in 1967, and his JD in 1970 from Georgetown University. He is Special Counsel to the American Society of Association Executives (ASAE), and he has served on the ASAE Board of Directors, headed its Government Affairs Committee, and founded its 1,000-attorney Legal Section. Books written or edited by Jacobs include *Association Law Handbook, Second Edition* (1986), *Association Issues* (1989), *Federal Lobbying Law Handbook, Second Edition* (1993), and *Certification and Accreditation Law Handbook* (1992).

David W. Ogden is Deputy General Counsel and Legal Counsel of the U.S. Department of Defense. Ogden received his BA, summa cum laude, in 1976 from the University of Pennsylvania, and his JD, magna cum laude, in 1981 from Harvard Law School. From 1982 to 1983, he served as a judicial law clerk to Associate Justice Harry A. Blackmun of the U.S. Supreme Court. He was formerly a partner of the Jenner & Block law firm and resident in its Washington office, where he litigated major constitutional and antitrust cases on behalf of associations in the health care and publishing fields; he also served as regular outside counsel to the ethics committee of a major health care professional association. Since 1991, Ogden has served as an Adjunct Professor of Law at Georgetown University Law Center.